COWBOY CORNER CONVERSATIONS

COWBOY CORNER CONVERSATIONS

Red Steagall

Edited by Loretta Fulton

State House
Press
McMurry University
Abilene, Texas

Library of Congress Cataloging-in-Publication Data

Steagall, Red.
    Cowboy corner conversations / Red Steagall; edited by
        Loretta Fulton.
    p. cm.
    ISBN 1-880510-84-7 (cloth : alk. paper)
    1. Cowboys--West (U.S.)--Interviews. 2. West (U.S.)--
Biography. 3. Ranch life--West (U.S.) 4. West (U.S.)--Social life and
customs. I. Fulton, Loretta. II. Title.
F596.S825 2004
978--dc22

                                                2004003514

State House Press
McMurry Station, Box 637
Abilene, TX 79697-0637
(325) 793-4682

Printed in the United States of America

ISBN 1-880510-84-7 cloth

This book is sposored in part by:

Book designed by Rosenbohm Graphic Design

CONTENTS

FOREWORD

Red Steagall has worn a lot of hats in his career. Some recall his time as a honky-tonk balladeer. Others know him as the official Cowboy Poet of Texas, as the consummate cowboy singer, as the leader of the best dance band in the state. To many he is the champion of things Western, rural, and agricultural.

I know Red as a historian. We first crossed paths when he came to play at a fund-raiser for the Buffalo Gap Historic Village, an outdoor museum I am helping to resuscitate and transform through the auspices of the McWhiney Foundation. At the time, I knew of him and his music only by reputation. After that first performance, I knew he was a fellow traveler.

His song and his bearing speak of a man who is a great showman. What I also discovered is that he is a dedicated preservationist, and a historian by avocation. Along with preserving bricks and mortar as we were doing at Buffalo Gap Historic Village, he also preserves the manner and mien, the music and the heart, of Western America. Not just black and white cowboys from the days of the open range, but Technicolor heroes from the silver screen, and flesh and blood people who are living the life and legacy left to us by those first inhabitants of the Great West.

Since that day in May of 2000, Red and I have been friends. His pioneering radio program, Cowboy Corner, is not only great entertainment, but is also one of the finest on-going oral history projects I have encountered in my career as a historian. The subjects of his interviews are important players—some famous, some behind the scenes—in the story of the West.

This book takes those same broadcast recordings—carried on radio stations across the nation—and recasts them as narrative. Together with so many others, we continue to preserve these uniquely American voices for generations to come.

Don Frazier
Abilene, Texas

INTRODUCTION

Ten years ago, I performed at a noon luncheon for the downtown Rotary Club of Fort Worth. In attendance was a car dealer friend, Mac Churchill. Mac really liked my poetry so he called his advertising agent, Stuart Balcom, and had Stuart contact me about doing a three-minute cowboy poetry show on WBAP radio five mornings a week.

I told Stuart that I didn't have any three-minute poems. He said, "How much time do you need?" I said, "At least thirty minutes." We then decided to do a demo of our show idea.

Stuart took the demo to the program director of WBAP who said that if we would do an hour show, he would air it (which he never did). We got excited. I then produced a one-hour demo and sent a copy to my dear friend, the late, great Mike Oatman at Great Empire Broadcasting in Wichita, Kansas. He and his partner, Mike Lynch, owned eleven stations at the time and they agreed to air "Cowboy Corner" on all their country stations.

Stuart, Mac and I then went to the bank and borrowed enough money to produce and market the show to the entire nation. We hired Ron Huntsman in Nashville, Tennessee, to clear stations for us and we went on the air in March of 1994 on 154 stations nationwide. Today, we're heard in 175 markets and growing.

In November of 1993, I was in Hawaii with my wife and some friends when I ran across an old and dear friend and his beautiful wife. Bob and Nan Kingsley were vacationing on the same island that we were. Bob hosts American Country Countdown—the largest syndicated radio show of any format. At the time, Nan was a very powerful force in radio time sales. They became the fourth part of our partnership and Nan provided us with a great slate of sponsors who have kept us running for the past ten years.

I thought, "Boy, if I can keep this show on the air for five years, we'll have hit a home run." As this book is printed, we are finishing our tenth year and are stronger than ever. We found a niche market that was accepting of the programming we have to offer and luckily no one told us that only one out of every three hundred show ideas ever makes it to syndication. We were in the right place at the right time with the right team.

I feel very fortunate to be able to interview folks who, every day, play a major part in preserving and perpetuating the history, traditions, heritage, and values of our Western way of life. In this book you'll read some of those interviews. There are a lot more and the list grows every day.

I'd like to take this opportunity to thank Loretta Fulton for all of the hard work that it took to transcribe these shows from tapes and CD's. She did a marvelous job.

Enjoy the comments from some of my dearest friends and some of our greatest heroes as we talk about the West and what it means. I hope you get as much joy out of the reading as I have gotten from the recording.

Thanks for trailing along with us. Hope you enjoy the ride.

Red Steagall

ROY ROGERS

On a windy day in Victorville, California, my son Carl and I arrived at the Roy Rogers Museum to spend some time with Roy for this interview. Even though I was acquainted with Roy, he was my childhood hero, and I was a little bit nervous. Carl was enthralled! I wanted to know about Roy's years growing up so I asked him if he ever dreamed of being a cowboy as a child. He answered this way:

I was raised on a farm in Ohio and did a lot of things cowboys do. I had a horse—my first horse was a mule. Then my dad got me a little ex-sulky racer named Babe. I was in seventh heaven when I got her—she'd outrun anything at the school or the church or anyplace.

I always liked music. On Saturday nights my cousins and my dad and I would get together and play the mandolin and guitars. My three sisters sang. That's the kind of family I remember. Those were the days when families loved families.

Did you really think about a career in music or were you just having fun?

We were just entertaining ourselves and our neighbors. I had three sisters, so we only had to get one more girl and three boys and we had a square dance.

When I was eighteen, I came to California to visit a sister I hadn't seen in six years. I stayed four months. I remember in the summer of 1931 I picked peaches.

I later went back to Ohio and then came back to California. I didn't have a job, so my sister said I ought to go see about getting on a program at a radio station in Inglewood. I was just an old country boy from the sticks, and I was bashful. She said, "Think of me when you're doing it." I did, but to this day I don't remember what songs I sang I was so scared.

A few days later I got a call asking me if I wanted to join the Rocky Mountaineers. There weren't any singers, just some guys playing instruments. We ran an ad in the newspaper and Bob Nolan answered it. That became the beginning of the Sons of the Pioneers.

We sang duets for a while and then ran some more ads. Tim Spencer answered, and the Sons of the Pioneers were a trio for a while. Then Hugh and Karl Farr joined us, and we got a sponsor. In 1934 we started making a few bucks, and it just went on from there.

When you started with the Sons of the Pioneers, did you guys just pack up in a car and travel over the country?

Yes, when we first started, the Sons of the Pioneers weren't getting any salaries. We would make personal appearances at clubs and play for midnight parties and dances. When we picked up enough money, we would tour all up and down California trying to make a few dollars.

Our records were getting pretty popular and we started getting some requests for working in pictures. We worked with Gene (Autry) in some of his pictures and Buck Jones. One day we were in Inglewood doing a show, and I went to pick up my hat. This guy walked in, all excited and said, "Can you get a cowboy hat in here?" I said I didn't know, I was just getting mine cleaned. He said he needed a cowboy hat for an eight o'clock screen test the next morning at Republic Studios.

I felt a little sneaky, but the next morning I went to Republic Studios myself. They wouldn't let me in without an appointment, so I sneaked in with a group of extras that were coming back from a restaurant across the street. I just got through the door and a hand fell on my shoulder. I said, "Oh, he's got me," and I turned around and this guy says, "Len, what are you doing here?" It was the producer of all Western pictures at that time. I was still Leonard Slye

Roy Rogers

then and he didn't know me as an individual, just as one of the Sons of the Pioneers. When I came through that door, that's what made him stop me.

He said he was looking for a new singing cowboy and asked me to come back to his office and sing a couple of songs for him. I was

Roy Rogers, center, with Red Steagall and Don Malone

scared to death. But I sang for him, and he said that was more like what he was looking for and asked me, "Are you tied up?"

I was. The Sons of the Pioneers and I had just signed up with Columbia Pictures, so I went to talk to the head of Columbia. He told me he would release me if the deal worked out with Republic, but I would have to find a replacement. I knew Pat Brady — he and his dad and another guy were working at a beer joint down by Long Beach — so the next day I drove down there. He was tickled to death to take over for me.

We worked out a deal at Republic, and I was under contract with them in another week or so. I signed up Oct. 13, 1937, and I made my first picture in December—*Under Western Stars*. We got off to a good start. Dust storms were covering the country, and new dams were being built to get more water. That was our story, too, and it turned out be timely and won best Western of the year.

Every boy in America had a stick horse or a real one named Trigger, so I naturally wanted to know about the most famous horse in the movie business: Roy, you had to have a horse, and you and I both knew Glenn Randall and admired his work. Is he responsible for finding Trigger for you?

No, Glenn came later. When they gave me the name Roy Rogers, they said I had to have a horse, too. A stable owned by Warner Brothers sent about eight of their cast horses out for me to try. Trigger was the third one I rode, and I never looked at the rest of them.

I made my first three or four pictures without owning him. We were advertised as Roy Rogers and Trigger, and when we made personal appearances, everyone asked where Trigger was. So I went to the stable and told them since it looked like I was going ahead with the picture business, I had to own a horse.

They hemmed and hawed a little bit and then said Trigger would cost $2,500. I liked to have died when he said $2,500—I didn't have 25 cents. But I raked up the money and bought him. He was in ninety feature shows and all 104 TV shows. He died when he was thirty-three. He was just a wonderful horse.

Who named him Trigger?

Smiley Burnette named him. We were doing a scene with some shooting and he made the remark "quick on the trigger" and said that's what I ought to name my horse. It was a good idea. He was fast — he could spin on a dime and give you ninety cents change.

Were you the first star to include the name of his horse in the headline with himself?

I don't remember anybody else. And when you think about cowboys, you just naturally think horses, too.

(Interviewed in 1994)

REBA McENTIRE

During the National Finals Rodeo of 1974 in Oklahoma City, I met the most talented and one of the sweetest girls I have ever known. She was singing the national anthem at the rodeo and then joined me in the Justin suite to sing some songs to a group of cowboys and cowgirls. I fell in love with her voice and her persona. I invited her and her mom Jackie to come to Nashville the next January and we cut a demo record. That fall we landed a deal for Reba with Mercury Records and the rest, so they say, is history.

I feel extremely fortunate to have been a little bit involved in her early career and then have the pleasure to watch her grow into one of the greatest vocalists and performers in the history of music, Broadway, and now, television and movies. She is a very special friend.

I was flattered when she agreed to do an interview for Cowboy Corner. And though I knew a lot about her family, I wanted the rest of the world to know, so I started the interview by asking her about the history of the McEntires:

We're an unusual breed. The more research I do the more amazed and enthused and bewildered I am with them, but mostly I'm entertained. Great-grandpap McEntire was a character. I don't know if everybody in the country liked him, but they tolerated him.

He lived in a "dutch oven" made out of rock and only him and his old dog would stay out there. It is rumored that he never once took a bath in his life. So, not only was he a colorful person, he probably smelled real good, too.

Reba McEntire

Reba McEntire at presentation of her first Gold Record; with Red Steagall, left,
Bruce Hinton, and Ralph Emory

My granddaddy settled around Sulphur and Ada. He lost the lease on his land and headed east. They stopped at Limestone Gap for the winter and liked it there. Daddy moved a little south and met Mama there, so they haven't been very far since they were born.

Your grandfather actually was the world's first champion steer roper, wasn't he?

I didn't know he was first, but Daddy told us if you won Cheyenne—the biggest rodeo of the year—you consequently were the world's champion. Grandpap won Cheyenne in '34.

Daddy won the world in '57, '58 and '61 in the Rodeo Cowboys Association. He spent a lot of time away trying to win enough money to buy the land they own today. He was a hard worker and instilled hard work and pride in all us kids. That's something I'm very, very proud of.

I've heard you say lots of times you guys really learned to sing going down the rodeo trail in the pickup, in the sleeper cabin.

It was really a car, an old Ford four-door. All four kids would get in the back seat and we'd head out to Cheyenne or West Texas or South Texas. We were used to wide open spaces, so once in a while we'd get to rasslin' a little bit and Daddy's arm would drop down off the back of the front seat.

He'd start pinching us a little bit, discipline us a little. But Mama took care of us. She'd get us to sing to keep us out of trouble. It was so unusual when we got back home. People would ask where we'd been. I guess we were the gypsies of the community because we traveled so much, but I sure was proud of Daddy. And you know, we learned geography, customs, ways of life and how people talked. It was truly an education.

I remember an incident that involved us both and was probably the most embarrassing time of my professional life. You and I were working together at the Copenhagen Skoal Super Stars Rodeo in Fort Worth. I want to hear your side of the story.

I remember your outfit was stunning. It was maroon, almost velvet. I thought of it as a riverboat gambler's outfit. It was really pretty and looked good on you. Before we went out you were hunting for a safety pin 'cause you said your zipper looked like it was fixing to break.

I don't remember if you found a safety pin, but when we came around the arena and dismounted, whatever you had holding your britches together gave way. We got to singing and you were in the spotlight. I looked up and your shorts were just shining right through. I couldn't get your attention. The crowd got tickled, and I thought you handled it real well.

I heard you say "Red, your fly's undone," so all I could do was turn around and let everybody see it 'cause I didn't want anybody to be cheated. You took my coat and tied the arms behind my back and we went on with the show.
We've talked about your grandpappy and your great-grandpappy. What about your grandmothers?

Daddy's mother died in 1950, and I was born in '55, but everyone talks very, very highly of her. She was kind-hearted and a school teacher. She taught first grade.

Where did your musical talent come from?

Mama's mama was a very spiritual woman. She loved the Lord and went to church every time the doors opened. The only time I heard her sing much was in the garden working the flowers, on the pond dam fishing, or when she was cooking or we were in church. So that was pretty much all the time.

Mama sings very well and has a great ear for music. I wish I had more of her instincts for it. I can sing sharp and not know it. We'd be practicing and call her in to hear us. She'd say, "Now that's perfect, do it again."

I remember that night at the Hilton Northeast in Oklahoma City. Your mother took me by the arm and asked if her little girl could come up to the Justin suite and sing with me. I'll never forget that night, and I'll always be grateful to her for doing that.
Most people don't realize what it takes to get to the point where you are now. And although there were some really good times, there were some tough times, too. But when you melt it all down into one little bitty pot, it was a wonderful experience, wasn't it?

I wouldn't trade it for the world. I remember you said to me, "I'm going to try to help you get away from some of the chug holes — I'll help you steer around them," and you have. You told me when I met you in 1974 that if I stuck with the right people I wouldn't get hurt because they would take care of me. And that's exactly what happened.

When you take your time, Reba, you learn to avoid all those pitfalls. And you also learn what's good for you and that's the important thing to me. You're not dictated to by the rest of the industry.

When I got over to MCA Records, I said I wanted to sing more country songs. I was doing more contemporary then. Jimmy Bowen told me I needed to find my own songs because nobody knew what I wanted to sing better than I did.

Now, when I talk to young ladies getting into the business the first thing I say is, "Work hard, don't bellyache, don't complain. Take the challenge, go after it. You get in there, you belly up to the bar, you do your hard work and you pay for it. And it always comes out better in the end."

Don't you think the best characteristic a person can have as far as success is concerned is perseverance and determination? Talent really comes second, doesn't it?

Oh, it's way down the line, really. Perseverance and hard work and determination.

Remember those days when you wanted it to happen so bad and you were trying to do everything you could to make it come together and it just wouldn't come together?

Yes, I remember, and I'd say, "Well, so and so didn't do as much as I did." Then a little voice in the back of my head would say, "Keep working, stay in there and the hard work will pay off." And it did.

(Interviewed in 1994)

BEN JOHNSON

It was my good fortune to know Ben Johnson. He was a special friend and one of the greatest men I have ever known. Everyone who knew him, loved him and we all called him Uncle Ben. His wife, Carol, was the perfect compliment to Ben. She was so kind and sweet. I loved her dearly.

I spent a lot of time with Ben as we raised money for children's charities through the Ben Johnson Celebrity ropings. The group that came together for those events, remains a very tight family and we all have become friends for life. It's a great group of actors, actresses, singers, stunt men, and professional ropers.

We all miss Ben very much but are thankful for the positive influence that he had on all of our lives. I was fortunate to get this interview shortly before Ben passed away.

I always like to find out a little bit about a person, so I asked Ben about his background.

I want you to tell the folks what part of the world you came from and how you got into the cowboy way of life.

Well, I came from Oklahoma. Back in about 1939 I was working on an old cattle ranch, the Chapman-Barnard outfit. Howard Hughes made a picture with Jane Russell called *The Outlaw.* He came to the ranch and bought a load of horses. He saw I could ride, so he hired me. That's how I got to Hollywood — in a car load of horses.

I've got a thing or two that I like to brag about. I am the only cowboy that ever won a world's championship in the rodeo and won an Oscar in the movies.

Ben Johnson and Red

When you were growing up in the Osage, your daddy was a cowboy, wasn't he?

Yes, sir, he was one of the first steer roping world champions. I always wanted to be a champion in something — playing marbles or something. I won a team roping championship in 1952, and it's been pretty good to me.

It's kind of like the old Oscar. Everybody thought I knew something after I won that, but I didn't know any more than I did before. However, I was a cowboy, I think, when I hit the ground. I knew how to ride a horse all my life. I started cowboyin' when I was about eleven, and when I wasn't going to school I was on the payroll.

The Chapman-Barnard was a couple hundred thousand acres in good strong country. They figured about ten acres to the head.

The Osage is always considered by cattlemen to be the primo cattle country on this whole planet. The main reason is that it's mostly limestone country with lots of spring water. The grass has lots of power in it.

What kind of horses did you ride and where did they come from?
Were they good animals?

Well, the cutting horses were pretty good horses, but the old everyday working horses—some of them were a little tough. You'd have to buck 'em out a little bit in the morning.

I started Lewis Brooks up there. We rode the rough string there for about two years. When he left, he went on rodeoing and he was the world's champion buckin' horse rider for two years. We got studs from the King Ranch, and they were pretty hot, a lot of them. But if an old horse bucked somebody off some other place, they'd go buy him and give him to us. So that's why I can't hardly walk now.

Knowing about Ben's Indian heritage, I got him to talk about it by stating that a lot of good Oklahoma cowboys have Indian blood in them, and I think that helps them be competitive. I always have felt that the Native Americans have a better feeling for animals than a lot of other folks do.

I think so too, Red. My mom's folks came up on the Trail of Tears out of Georgia—they were Cherokee people. My dad came from Arkansas, and when he was just a kid he came to the Osage area and stayed there the rest of his life.

Did you just work as a wrangler for a while in Hollywood—you
didn't just start off being an actor, did you?

No, when they had a chase to do, I would go double somebody. It was pretty good to me. Howard Hughes put me in the picture business. I went under contract to John Ford, and that's when I started doing some of his movies.

Then, I was doubling Henry Fonda in *Fort Apache*. There was a munitions wagon turned over and they had three actors in it. I ran in and got the team stopped, and nobody got hurt. Ford said, "Ben, you'll be well rewarded for this." About a week later, he called me into the office and handed me an envelope. He said, "Have your lawyer read this." Well, it wasn't sealed, so I opened it. It was a seven-year contract. Down about five or six lines, it went to $5,000 a week, and that's as far as I read. I got that pen, and I signed it and gave it back.

*Ben Johnson, second from right, with cowboy artist Bill Owen,
cowboy poet Baxter Black, and Red*

***I remember a story that you told me about something that hap-
pened as you rode out of an arena one time. Tell us about it.***

Lots of things come along to tell you that you're not too great. I
had won the world in the team roping in 1952. I went to Denver and
got my big new saddle and big shiny belt buckle.

The next show was Phoenix. The announcer tells everybody what
a great roper I am, the world's champion, and I never miss. I was
going to show everybody how great I was, so I got this old steer.

When I came out I didn't even hit him in the hind end with it.
I rode out the back of the arena and headed for the cold drink stand.
I heard this little voice hollering, "Hey, mister." This little guy, about
five or six years old, looks up at me and says, "How in the hell did you
ever get to be a world champion?"

***Had you already started in the movies when you decided
to go for the world?***

Well, yes. At that time I was under contract to John Ford. I just quit the picture business, which was kind of a foolish thing to do. But it was pretty good to me, and I won the world championship.

***Ben, at that time, there were several other cowboys involved
in the motion picture business, so if you got out on the road and
got all that publicity, that couldn't do anything but make the
movie companies look at you harder.***

Well it made things a lot easier and put you in a position where you could pick and choose, really. I liked to make something decent you could take your family to see.

***When you returned to Hollywood after the world championship,
how did the movie industry accept you after your absence?***

I stayed on the road almost the whole year. When I won the world championship, I drove in the driveway and said, "Honey, I'm the world's champion." And she said, "Have you got any money?" I said, "I've got a big new saddle and a shiny belt buckle," and she said, "We can't eat that."

From then on I went back into the picture business and stayed in it ever since.

Let's talk about the first big picture you were in.

Well, the ones I had the lead in were *Mighty Joe Young* and *Wagon Master*. Then *She Wore a Yellow Ribbon, Rio Grande, Shane,* just every good Western you could think of, I was in it somewhere.

How did The Last Picture Show ***come about? I know you had a
little bit of a struggle with it in the beginning.***

Yes I did. They sent me a script, and I read it and it was the worst thing I ever read, I thought, because of all the dirty words, and I turned it down. They offered me everything in the world, and I kept turning it down.

I took another job down in Houston and one day John Ford called and asked if I would do him favor. I said, "Yes sir," before I asked what it was. He wanted me to do *The Last Picture Show*.

I knew they had me, so I called the director, and I told him I would do it if he would let me rewrite my part and do it for a salary—I didn't want a percentage in an old dirty movie.

They let me rewrite it, and I won the American Academy Award, the English Academy Award, the Golden Globe Award, the People's Award and the New York Critics' Award, and I didn't have to say one dirty word.

***Ben, I was in the airport not long ago and a young man came
by me with a couple of girls and using the foulest language
I believe I've ever heard. And that just kind of translates
from our society to the screen.***

You know I don't believe they have the ability to express themselves. I believe that's what's the matter—they didn't get the right kind of milk when they were little.

(Interviewed in 1996)

J.J. GIBSON

J.J. Gibson made a major difference in my life. He not only was as good a friend as I have ever had or ever will have, but he gave me an opportunity to experience the cowboy way of life in a way I had never seen it. He invited me to the Four Sixes (6666) branding twenty-seven years ago and, as of this writing, I have not missed a year since.

Because of his generosity, plus that of the owner, Mrs. Anne Marion, and the friendship of J.J.'s son Mike (general manager of the Four Sixes), I still continue to experience the language, the skills, the geography, and the ethics of the cow country of West Texas. Besides all that I am very fortunate to have some Four Sixes horses in my string.

J.J.'s widow, Naida, his sons, Jim and Mike, and Mike's family—Shanda and their two lovable sons P.L. and J.J.—continue to impact my world in a very positive way. I will always be indebted to J.J. Gibson and we all miss him dearly.

Before he passed away, I had the opportunity to talk to him about his background and the ranching industry of West Texas.

My family originated in Tennessee. After the War Between the States, my grandfather brought his family to Texas in about 1872, stayed in Tarrant County a few years and then settled in Young County in 1879. The land is now part of Possum Kingdom Lake.

My Uncle John came out here in 1883. My father and his brother, Lee Gibson, came here about the same time, and Lee was appointed sheriff of King County when it was organized in 1892. John had a

J. J. Gibson and Red

general store. When the Burnetts bought the ranch they bought him out, and the store turned out to be the Four Sixes supply house.

My Uncle Lee homesteaded on some land next to the Pitchfork. He had a dugout and was digging a well there for water when it caved in on him and killed him. He left a widow and four children. He was twenty-eight years old. His wife and children moved to the Vernon area.

My dad also had a homestead. He brought his two older brothers from Young County in the spring of 1886 when he was sixteen years old. In those days when you were sixteen you were on your own. He went up the trail toward Guthrie, and when he came to Seymour he asked about work out in the Western country. They told him about Uncle Isom Lynn, a settler here and an old Indian fighter who came out here in 1877 with the first cattle in King County.

So he asked Uncle Isom Lynn if he could follow him out toward Guthrie because he didn't know the way. Uncle Isom Lynn was a racehorse enthusiast, and he'd gotten beat in a race in Seymour. He wasn't very happy about it, so he tied that race horse behind his buggy and headed home. And he didn't stop until he got down in the eastern part of King County in what we call Little Arizona.

By this time it's about twelve o'clock at night. So he stopped and turned around to my father and said, "Kid, you see that North Star— you go about fifteen miles straight north of here and you'll find the JF Headquarters, and I think you can get work there." He turned around and hit that horse over the butt with his bridle reins and left dad there, so he didn't have any choice.

If you've never been in eastern King County, it's the roughest part of the county, and here that sixteen-year-old boy was. He rode until he judged he'd come fifteen miles. It was almost daylight. He hollered right loud, and in a minute heard a pistol shot. And so he had come that close to the JF Ranch, and he started out his cattle punching there. This was in '86 and he worked there until 1890 and went over to what's the Four Sixes today.

When he first came here, who owned the Four Sixes?

It was Eastern money—the Louisville Land and Cattle Co. out of Louisville, Kentucky.

When I took over managing the Four Sixes in 1970, I found a letter in the desk written to Mr. J.W. Arnett, who at that time was the manager of the Old Eights. The letter was from the general manager in Louisville, Kentucky, dated 1892. He asked Mr. Arnett to meet him in Seymour on a certain date.

The interesting thing about the letter was, they were talking about the same problems we talk about today—grass and water and the prospect of purchasing some more cattle when he got there. Mr. Arnett then became the first foreman of the Four Sixes.

You told me your dad lived in a dugout when he first came. Did he build it?

No, it served as a camp for the Louisville Land and Cattle Co. My son, Mike, has hunted around there and found some rifle hulls and things like that that proved the camp was there.

Boy, that must have been a pretty lonely life.

Red, they had a job—they were making a living, and you were doing pretty good in those days if you could do that.

They suffered untold hardships. I don't know how they got through the winters. I know a horse fell on my daddy once and broke his collarbone. He rode sixty miles on horseback to Quanah to get the bone set. I don't know if anybody could do that today.

Up there on that piece of land your daddy homesteaded, there's some vats up there. What were they originally designed for?

My father was working here when the Burnetts bought the ranch, and Mr. Arnett had my dad oversee building the vat that is now called the Gibson pens vat. There weren't any ticks in this country until they brought the cattle here from Indian Territory where the Burnetts were pasturing their cattle.

That was the reason for that vat. All the cattle that came here had to be driven all the way to Gibson pens and dipped. That's the way they handled the tick problem. We used them up until recent years. It's gotten cost-prohibitive to use them nowadays.

(For folks who don't know what a dipping vat is, it was a long trough a little bit deeper than the cattle were tall, so the cattle had to swim. They were completely immersed in this solution of pesticide and water. You'd run them off in one end, they'd swim to the other and they were drenched to kill the ticks.

In the early days one thing that stopped the cattle drives, even before they fenced the country off, was the ticks that the cattle brought up from South Texas. They were immune to tick fever, but the cattle north of the Red River weren't immune to it. Thousands and thousands of them died from tick fever, so until they learned about using those dipping vats it was really a problem.)

After we got rid of the ticks, we used them for lice control and just our regular old cedar ticks, which are different from the fever ticks.

J.J., I know how important horses are to you, and I want to talk a little bit about the Hancock blood that was introduced to the Four Sixes horses in the early years. Is it still prevalent?

It's been bred out to a certain extent, but in recent years I re-introduced it. They're horses with a lot of heart. They've got good bone, they've got good legs on them, they don't cripple easy, and they've got good minds.

Why is it important to let the Hereford cows keep their horns?

It seems like when you take the horns off, you domesticate them a little bit, and we've all been guilty of domesticating our cattle too much nowadays. We just think they're mothers and can protect their calves better from the coyotes if they've got their horns on them.

Cowboys like them for the way they work—they don't bunch up so much. They drive easier and move easier. It may seem a little old-timey, but some of the old-timey ways are still good.

Tell us about when the Indians would come down from Oklahoma and Mr. Burnett would give them beef.

Oh, yes. Mr. Burk Burnett became good friends with Quanah Parker when they were leasing the Indian Territory. When it was opened up for settlement, that's the reason he bought this ranch in 1898. Mr. Burnett told the Indians that he would furnish them beeves for the winter for as long as he lived over there.

That practice continued until the mid-1930s. I was a little boy, and my father took me over to that Indian camp where they killed beeves and cut it up to dry it out to take it back to the reservation. I had a very vivid memory of those Indians over there.

I was fortunate to get in on the tail end of that generation. My father was a real pioneer out here in this country, and I just got into this world in time to see a little bit of it.

How about your early days on the Four Sixes?

I went to work for the Four Sixes in 1946 when I had just gotten out of the Marines in World War II. I came out here and went to the wagon. There were five or six of us single boys and that was our home. We didn't have any other place to live.

George Humphrey, the manager then, was prominent in the Texas Cowboy Reunion in Stamford and that was our big deal. Or maybe the Old Settlers up at Roaring Springs. But there wasn't many breaks—it was pretty well seven days a week.

Tell us the story about when you were a little boy and George was sheriff of King County.

I was about twelve years old and my brother and I were riding on the ranch and ran into a still—it scared us to death. So we got George and led him to it. He told us to stay under a cedar tree while he went in and got 'em out. We stayed under that cedar tree it seemed like nearly all night. George finally came back and said, "Boys, they loaded up and got away."

Many, many years later I found out those were some of George's buddies who had that still, and he just went in and visited with them and came back and told us they got away.

There are a lot of young people out there who think they would like to be cowboys. Is it still as romantic a life as people think it is?

Well, the romance is pretty well gone out of it, really. To be a cowboy today, a person has got to be real dedicated   it's not an easy life. I tell the young people who come here to Guthrie, there's no social life here to speak of. We do have a church and a school here. You just have to be a real dedicated person, because it's not going to be a big monetary reward. It's a way of life.

Did you have dances in West Texas when you were young?

I remember them right here in Guthrie. When my wife and I were going together, we used to go to the dances on Saturday night at the school. They had a big ol' pot-bellied stove.

You have your own ranch now. Part of it's been in your family since the 1800s. You told me one time you were going to retire, but I haven't seen you retire yet.

I don't want to retire. I'm very happy as the general manager of the Burnett Ranches. Mike does the day-to-day operation, I run the feedlot operation and help him with the buying and selling.

Your son, Mike, has a very strong ranching heritage. Your wife's
family has been in the ranching business a long time, too.

Yes, her grandfather and his father, W.Q. Richards and T.J. Richards, they had a lot of country in the early days.

Well, I can tell you, J.J., some of the greatest memories of my
life have been standing out on these bluffs with you early in
the morning talking about the ranch and the West and
the cattle business. Those are times I'll never forget.

Red, if you can't get your priorities straight along about that time of day when you see the sun coming up and the cowboys bringing those cows around, you've got a problem.

(Interviewed in 1995)

REX ALLEN

As I was growing up, I had several cowboy heroes. One of them was Rex Allen. Then, as I started getting into the entertainment business, I had several role models. Again, one of those role models was Rex Allen. I admired and respected him very much, and I was fortunate to become his friend. I remember those times at his ranch in Malibu when I would just listen entranced to that golden voice tell me about his experiences in show business.

In later years, we did a lot of shows together, including farm progress shows throughout the Midwest. I have been on stage several times with his son, Rex, Jr. Rex, Jr. is an accomplished showman and gentleman just like his dad. Rex, Sr. had a tremendous influence on me and I'll always be grateful for his guidance and friendship.

I caught him one day in Tucson and started our interview by asking about his background.

I was born and raised around Wilcox, Arizona, and went through high school there. Then I became a citizen of the world. When I was in Chicago I wrote *Arizona Cowboy*. Then when I got to Hollywood they decided that should be the name of my first movie, which was a turkey. I had to find the negative and burn that one.

You know you're very fortunate to have any movies.
Think of all the millions of people who would give anything
in the world to do that.

Rex Allen

Yeah, we were sitting one day—Tex Ritter, Gene Autry, Roy Rogers, and me—yakking about this and that. Gene had gotten out of Republic and got out on his own. Roy just left Republic for TV. I'd only been there two or three years.

Ritter sat there listening to us talking about getting out. Then he looked at all of us and said, "How do you get *in*?" Tex was a great guy, just a wonderful friend. Somebody told me I would meet a lot of people, but they said if you run into anybody who goes to running down Tex Ritter or Tex Williams, "look out for him, there's something wrong with him."

I'd like to know a little bit more about where you came from.

My dad was raised around San Angelo and came to Arizona the year Arizona became a state. My grandmother was born in Wilcox, went back to Texas, got married, and then came back. My great-grandfather drove the stagecoach between Tombstone and Wilcox and Lordsburg. And now I'm back in Arizona, I'm home.

You have left a legacy to this world of music and movies and entertainment that no one will ever duplicate because that was uniquely Rex Allen. I think what the world will remember most of all is that wonderful melodious voice.

You think so? I've said several times, Red, that this country has been so beautiful to me that when I go, it's gonna take them six months to wipe the smile off my face before they can lay me out.

Tell us a little bit about how you got into the movies.
How did that transition take place?

The funny thing is, I never had any ambitions to do that. I just wanted to try to make a living singing if I could. When I had a few pretty good hit records, enough to give me a national identification, Paramount Pictures called. They said they had a new Hopalong Cassidy series and needed a singing cowboy. We talked back and forth for a couple of months, and then it just kind of faded out.

Then Gene Autry was starting a production house and he called me. He had a series he wanted to do, and he sent me a contract. I backed out, and then Roy Rogers came to town. He was leaving Republic for Fox and wanted to do a series. He and I talked for a year.

One Sunday morning a guy called and said he owned Republic Pictures and wanted to talk to me. He wanted me to come down to his hotel the next morning for breakfast, so I called Roy and asked him who the guy was. It all worked out, and that's how it happened.

Tell us about your song, "Queen of the Rodeo."

Well, I was living in Chicago working at WLS radio, and all the publishing firms were going to increase their charges to the radio stations. For two weeks we had to do nothing but old folk songs and things that the copyright had run out on.

So I started writing songs. I had a thirty-minute show, and I'd write two new songs at night and bring them in. "Queen of the Rodeo" was one of them. A lot of the girl singers are singing that now.

The image of the cowboy and his horse is one of the most vivid images to people all over the world. I know there was a horse that was very special in your career.

There was just one. I never could find a double for him. Koko was ten years old when I bought him. I saw that big long white mane and tail blowing in the wind, and I thought that had to be the prettiest horse I ever saw in my life. He died when he was twenty-nine, and I used him until he was about twenty-six. I'd put two feet of straw in that trailer, and he'd lay down to travel. We were playing lots of rodeos at that time.

I miss those days. I couldn't do it now, but at the time I was doing it I looked forward to it. They were beautiful days — just a great time of my life. The cowboys ended up being better friends of mine than I ever had in the picture business. They were square-shootin' wonderful guys.

I don't think there's a finer group of people anywhere in the world than the folks who make their living with rodeo. Don't you believe it's because each one is an individual? It's not a team sport.

Oh yeah, Red, you sang a song about Freckles Brown. When Freckles first started, he wasn't traveling with anybody. Lots of times, Freckles would come to my room the last night of the rodeo to tell me he didn't have enough to get to the next place. He'd ask if it was all right if he rode with Koko.

He would help drive and clean the stalls and all that stuff. He was one of the greatest guys I have ever known in the rodeo business or anywhere else.

I don't want to dwell on this, but you really are my hero. You did all the things in show business that I always wanted to do. I've always wanted to ask you how you got hooked up with Disney to do the voice-over for those wonderful pictures.

When I first went to Hollywood, the studio would try to help you build your name. There was a big function that my wife and I went to. We were seated at the table with Walt Disney. I was just in awe of him. After two hours, he asked if I had ever narrated any films, and truthfully I didn't know what he was talking about. He said they did a lot of nature and animal films and asked me to come by and take a look at them. I beat him to the studio.

He liked what I did. Now I've done over two hundred of them. It was a great relationship. He was kind of like a dad to me. He told me that if what the writer had written didn't fit me, then to just say whatever I wanted to. He never changed a word.

(Interviewed in 1996)

JIGGS MANN

Jiggs Mann is a good cowboy. Any man will tell you that he'd love to have Jiggs Mann ride his horses and work his cattle. I have known Jiggs for a long time and I always enjoy his company and I love to hear his stories about the JA and the Palo Duro Canyon.

We were camped at the Battle Creek Pens when I asked Jiggs, "Where did you pitch camp when you worked this pasture?" He answered, "Right over there about forty yards. It's a good camp, but we stayed here three weeks. This pasture was 38,000 acres."

I asked Jiggs about his early life.

I was raised just south of here right next to the JA Ranch, and I've been here ever since except for a couple of years in the service. Evelyn and I married in '55, and we left there for two or three years and then we came back.

How old were you when you went to work on the JA ?

I went there in about '45 and worked summers while I was in school. But I didn't go to work steady there until 1947. I worked there 'til '50 and then went to the service and came back. I ran the ranch for about ten years and then left. Then I got a lease out there. I've just kind of been around it all my life.

In those early days, we did everything on horseback. There was a windmill wagon and an old truck. They took care of everything you had to do. The foreman had a Ford car. Until we got the Jeeps after the war, that was just about it.

Jiggs Mann, center, with Red and cowboy artist Bruce Greene

How big was the ranch?

Clear over there by Silverton—I don't know how far that was, but it was a long way. I think we branded about five thousand calves or something like that. Just about the time I went in there, from '47 on, they started selling off the country. We were cleaning out all that country on the Palo Duro. We had lots of wild cattle to catch and haul 'em out.

A lot of folks don't know where the JA is, and I think it's important we tell them because Palo Duro Canyon has some of the most dramatic and beautiful country you've ever seen.
Tell the folks a little bit about chasing those wild cattle out of there.

You didn't think much about it then. Our best time of year to go in was March. The cattle were weaker then after winter. You could make one big run at them, and that was all of it. The rest of the time they'd be run down pretty good. We had some horses that would go faster through that brush than I wanted to go. They'd get you up there pretty quick.

Lots of time we'd make a stand down in the bottom of the creek. When they'd come off those big points, we'd be lined up here ready to get 'em, and the race would be on. Those were beautiful cattle. If you didn't handle them just right, they'd die. Most of the time those old men would teach us how to handle them, and we didn't lose too many of them.

Tell us about the horses the JA had when you were there.

Well, we had horses from the King Ranch and Waggoner's and later on from R.A. Brown in Throckmorton. I believe the best horses I rode all around there were the King Georges from the King Ranch. But it took all of them to make it work. They'd pick two men out of the outfit who'd break those horses. They weren't that bad. If you could get on 'em and keep going, you'd be all right.

They'd last longer than you'd think. You started them at four-year-olds and they were mature. Unless something happened, they'd go 'til they were fifteen or sixteen years old.

Did each cowboy shoe his own horses?

Yeah, there'd be some of them that didn't like to do it, and they'd do a little trading. I enjoyed shoeing a horse, you know, to make it look good.

I want to talk more about the wagon. That's the romantic part of this life as far as people looking on from the outside. Was it really as romantic and as neat as it looked like it was?

Why, I believe it was. I'd like to go through it again. It was quite a deal. When I was a kid and got out of school I couldn't wait to get to that wagon. I wouldn't even wait to pick up my report card. Yeah, it was a wonderful life. It had some hard times to it, but I enjoyed it very much. I wish I had kept a diary.

At the JA's, we would start off in the evening. We'd catch horses about six o'clock. We'd catch a stake horse and that's the one we'd make the drive on. We'd stake that horse and then everybody would go to bed pretty early because after dark there wasn't nothing else to do. We'd be up early the next morning. You'd get your horse saddled first, and then you'd eat breakfast and head out to make one of these drives. Then when we'd come in at night, the horse wrangler would be there with his remuda, and many men would jump down and get ropes around those horses. We'd catch us out a roundup horse and then put those cattle in a trap.

We didn't do too much in the evening because it would get so hot down there on that river. Lot of times us boys in the evening we'd catch us a horse and go up to the head of the canyon and run those cattle out of there.

I'll always regret that when I was a kid I didn't pay much attention to the old people. I was always watching a good bronc rider or good roper. But those old men, if you'd just watch 'em you could learn a lot of things. If I had it to do over, I'd go back and watch those old men, and I'd learn something.

A lot of us who write cowboy songs find ourselves writing a lot about old cowboys. I got to thinking it's because we're a family-oriented society. We look at older cowboys, not only as teachers, but as grandfather figures.

They were your idols. You'd watch them and respect their judgment and hear what they had to say. They were good people. I wish we had a lot of them here today.

When you came in during the winter time, you stayed in the bunkhouse. Was it that romantic or was it just a bed and a floor and four walls?

That was it, a bed and a floor and four walls. We read a lot. Ever now and then an old boy would have a radio, and we'd play that. We played lots of penny ante poker. If you was a big winner you wouldn't have over two dollars, but it was something to consume the time.

When we'd get out on the flat country out of the canyon, some of us would have transportation and we'd make a run for town. You didn't think about it being a lonely life. That was just the way it was.

(Interviewed in 1994)

ELMER KELTON

Elmer Kelton is my favorite Western writer. His characters are so compelling. They jump off the page at me and come to life. Maybe it's because I grew up in West Texas and know people like the ones he writes about. Or maybe it's because he's so historically correct that intrigues me. Whatever it is, Elmer Kelton will forever be remembered as one of the great storytellers of all time. I'm so proud that he's my friend, and I am constantly looking forward to his next new book.

I interviewed Elmer in his home surrounded by an enormous collection of Western books. I asked him how he got started writing novels.

I knew by the time I was eight or nine years old I wanted to write because I loved to read so much. I got serious about it after I came back from World War II. I began writing short stories in college and sending them off to Western pulp magazines. I wasn't having any success, but I was getting a lot of experience. I sold one my last semester, and I thought then it was going to be real easy. But it was a year after that before I sold my second. I wrote short stories and novelettes for seven or eight years before I tackled a novel. My first one was *Hot Iron,* which was based loosely on cattle ranching in the Panhandle.

I grew up in Upton County. My dad was foreman of the McElroy Ranch and later general manager. It was just natural that I was always more interested in things more Western. I came out to San Angelo to take a job as agriculture reporter on the local newspaper. I

Elmer Kelton, right, with Baxter Black, Don Blasingame, and Red

was going to take it on a temporary basis, thinking since I already sold one short story I was on my way to becoming rich and famous. It took a little longer than I thought—I remained an agriculture writer for forty-two years.

But I enjoyed being out among ranch and farm people. Those were the people I knew from the time I was old enough to know anything. Very often I feel the characters in my historicals are probably the grandparents of some of the people I know.

When I talk to people out in the hinterlands, they always talk about The Time It Never Rained. *Let's talk about that book.*

This was a book I wrote about the drought of the 1950s. Actually, I wrote it three times. During the drought, I was a reporter for the *San Angelo Standard-Times*, and this drought was my daily running story for seven years.

During the drought, I got to thinking what a great background it would be for a novel. After it ended in 1957, I wrote a version of it and sent if off to New York. Nothing came of it, so I wrote it again from scratch. Nobody was interested in it, so I just put it away for about ten years while I wrote more conventional Westerns.

Finally, after I had had my first big hardcover book, *The Day the Cowboys Quit*, my editor asked me what I would do next. I dug that story out and rewrote it from page one and sent it in. I think of all the novels I have written since then, that's the only one they didn't change a word in.

Let's talk a little bit about The Day the Cowboys Quit.

It was based on the Tascosa cowboy strike in 1883. The corporate mentality had moved into the big ranches in Panhandle. Distant owners were trying to run ranches like factories back East. One ranch had big lists of rules and tacked them on the bunkhouse walls. Cowboys were used to their freedom, so they decided to strike.

Several cowboys were involved, and they thought they'd have the ranchers to their knees in no time. But the ranchers brought in cowboys from other places, and the strike more or less disintegrated in about a month.

But in the long run, the ranchers lost, too. The cowboys stayed as settlers and storekeepers, and their presence helped encourage more immigration. The first thing the big ranchers knew, they had lost political control of those Panhandle counties.

Tell us about another book based in the Panhandle called Slaughter. *Did you base that on John Cook's account?*

Yes, I used his account for some of the background, and books by buffalo hunters and an article by J. Wright Mooar. He and his brother started the buffalo slaughter because they found an outlet for the raw buffalo hides. When a New York leather merchant found a way to tan them, it opened up a whole new market. Within a period of just a very few years, it just almost totally decimated the whole western buffalo herd. The real slaughter started about 1871 or 1872 in Kansas and Nebraska and moved to Texas in 1873 and '74. By 1880 you would have to say the buffalo herd was pretty well gone all over the West.

Let's talk about* The Wolf and the Buffalo, *one of my favorites.

It's based on the story of the black cavalry in Texas and the Comanche Indians in their last days as free-roaming horse Indians. It was an assignment from somebody else. *Reader's Digest Condensed Books* wanted a story about black cowboys in the West. I dreamed up an Indian character, too, and he began to take about half the book.

There were quite a few black soldiers in this part of the world. The Indians called them the Buffalo Soldiers. There were two regiments of cavalry, the Ninth and the Tenth, and two regiments of infantry. The Ninth was stationed at Fort Concho in San Angelo a time or two, but the Tenth had its headquarters at Fort Concho for the better part of ten years. They transferred to Fort Davis when the Comanche problems were pretty well taken care of, but the Apaches were still pretty much on the loose in West Texas, New Mexico and Arizona.

We didn't learn a lot about the buffalo soldiers when we were growing up because Texas was still pretty well a segregated state. But it's amazing how the fabric of this part of the world is colored with all different kinds of folks.

The old image of Texas was the white Anglo-Saxon cowboy on horseback. But if you look at Texas, we had great waves of immigration especially from Western Europe. But there were also slaves. The Hispanics and Indians were here all along. Texas was a big melting pot.

I really like* The Good Old Boys. *Tell us how much of a thrill it was to sit down in front of the television set and see that translated to the screen with Tommy Lee Jones.

It was quite a thrill. I can't say I had much to do with the movie. Tommy Lee Jones wrote his own script, but he followed the book very closely. When I wrote the book, maybe I didn't envision the characters quite the way they showed up on the screen, but from now on that's the way they're going to be.

I thought he did an absolutely wonderful job, and it's one of my all-time favorite movies. He said he didn't make any money off that one. He just did it because he wanted to. So many times those are the ones that have the most heart and the longest life.

That's true. You know, some of John Ford's greatest movies were the ones that lost money. But they're the ones that have endeared themselves to people because they were done out of love and not for money.

What's your favorite book you've written?

I'd have to say most of the time *The Time It Never Rained.* Occasionally, I might say *The Good Old Boys.* Both those books were real personal to me. They came out of things I saw and people I knew, old family stories and so forth.

Will James endeared himself with **Smoky the Cow Horse.** *It caused young people who read it to run off and go West. What's your image of a guy like Will James?*

I discovered him in grade school. Will James, Zane Grey and J. Frank Dobie were probably my three most prominent inspirations. I loved Will James and tried to copy his style.

Did you ever meet Mr. Dobie?

I used to see him on the campus of the University of Texas. I would want to go up and introduce myself, then I'd stop myself. I didn't do it, and I've regretted it ever since. He came along at a time when so many of those old-timers were a little past their prime, maybe, but still had sharp and clear memories. I knew a few of the old-timers when I was a little kid, but I wasn't ready to learn all those things from them. I was fascinated by their stories, but I didn't take any notes. What I have in my memory is mostly the spirit of the stories, not the details.

How about J. Evetts Haley?

He was pretty much of a historian rather than a folklorist. His book about Charles Goodnight is the best written about the cattle industry. He was a tremendous influence on me trying to find my own way.

Well, you have found your way, Elmer. In the next generation, somebody will ask the same question I just asked you. You'll be in that list of greats. There's no doubt in my mind.

(Interviewed in 1996)

JIM SHOULDERS

I have known Jim Shoulders for close to thirty years. I feel very fortunate to call him my friend. Jim not only is the winningest cowboy in the history of rodeo, he has also had a tremendous impact on the sport as a whole.

When most of the cowboys of his time were treating rodeo as a game, Jim treated it as a business. He was dedicated to providing a future for himself and his family. He has been used as an example of sportsmanship, business, and dedication by a large number of people in the great American sport of rodeo.

His wife, Sharon, is one of the kindest and sweetest people I have ever known. Gail and I both consider her a very special friend. Their children have all made a place for themselves in society and are pillars of their community. The whole world of rodeo is a better place because Jim Shoulders came our way.

I asked Jim to tell us a little bit about his early background.

I was born and raised on acreage about ten miles east of Tulsa, Oklahoma. My dad was an automobile body repairman. He pumped some wells and then got into the body repair business. When I was little I wanted to be a fender-pounder, but I got started going to some rodeos with my older brother.

We always had a horse and milked a couple of cows and raised a few pigs to eat. It was during the war and all the able-bodied young fellows were in the Army or the defense plants, and I got a job of shocking oats and wheat for twenty-five cents an hour.

Jim Shoulders

I went to a rodeo and got in the bull riding. I remember they were riding Hereford bulls and Brahman cows in the bull riding. We like to got killed, trying to get the Hereford bulls into the chutes so we wouldn't have to get on those hooking cows back behind us. I ended up winning $18, and I thought I'd never see another poor day, especially when you compare that to twenty-five cents an hour for ten hours a day in the wheat field.

In 1945 I went to Houston and entered the bull riding. They made me join the Cowboy Turtle Association with my $10 worth of eating money. Then, before the rodeo was over, they had a general meeting in the coliseum and voted to change the name to the Rodeo Cowboys Association. I got to hold my hand up and vote, so I was pretty proud they took my $10.

I was sixteen when I went to Houston. I don't know if I was the youngest one who voted, but I probably was the brokest one anyway. I was still going to school and had gotten out of class to go to Houston for ten days. I really suspect I was the youngest guy who voted to change the name. I won my first world's championship in 1949.

The Turtle Association was the first time the cowboys organized as a group. At the biggest rodeos, or in all rodeos, they made contestants pay an entry fee, but it wasn't added to the purse. A lot of times if you had fifty guys entered and they paid $20 each, that's $1,000 but the prize money wouldn't be $500. The cowboys wanted the entry fees added to the purse, which was no more than fair.

They went on strike at Boston Garden, and the producers tried to get some guys from that area to compete. It might have worked a little better for the producers if they had struck in Texas or Oklahoma or Wyoming where they could have had a shot to get some cowboys. But it was a little harder to get replacement cowboys in Boston.

The story goes that they were going to move ahead real slow like a turtle, so they just called it the Cowboy Turtle Association, and it stuck until 1945 at Houston. They got into a little copyright conflict with RCA Victor so they added "Professional" to make it PRCA.

Today there's something like well over ten thousand members and that many associate members. The original signers were less than a hundred.

Jim, rodeo is uniquely American. I think that's the thing that's important to me—it was born and bred in America and it is still second only to football. That says a lot for the sport.

Everyone says it's tougher to get a ticket to the National Finals Rodeo than it is to the Super Bowl. It's really a tough ticket.

When you got on bulls the first time, do you think they were the same caliber bulls we see in rodeo today?

The best of them were like the best of them now. The difference now is there are so many more of them. There's herds of those rank bulls.

There was a time you would go to Madison Square Garden and Everett Colburn had the best string. He always had a bunch of rank bulls. I'm sure they would fit right in the eliminator pen at the National Finals today, but he also had another thirty or forty lesser bulls.

There's fewer really good horses now and ten times as many really good bulls as there were back when I started in the '40s.

There was a time when you went north you never saw a bull or a cow or anything with much ear, but now they run a lot of Brahman-cross cattle even in Canada. This is the real difference for the fact that it's nothing for a bull to bring $30,000 if he's really a rank bull. It's because of the TV coverage. Money still talks.

As a young cowboy from Oklahoma, going to New York City must have been an experience that you never dreamed of.

Sharon and I got married in September of 1947, and I had won a little money and had a pretty good summer at the rodeos around. I said I've got enough money for us to get back home on. I went to New York and lucked out and won the bareback bronc riding and the bull riding. Some of them say it's the only time in history anyone's won two events there.

For a kid a year out of high school, I won about $5,000, and consequently it was probably a bigger win or bigger thrill for me to win New York that first time than either my first world's championship or my last one or what. I didn't really have that much confidence I could beat that caliber of contestants just a year out of high school, but I lucked out and won.

It was fifty-four performances in New York in twenty-nine or thirty days. It was pretty good experience for me starting out rodeoing, but I almost lost my wife. I rode a bull, they said, and I got down on the side and he knocked me out. They hauled me to the first aid stand, and when I came to I didn't know where I was or anything. When I woke up the next morning, I looked over at Sharon and said, "Who are you and what the hell are you doing in my bed?"

Needless to say, she jumped up and ran out and was scared to death. My friends kept coming by to see me and I kept saying, "What happened?" They kept telling me I was chasing the maid and fell down the elevator shaft. They kept telling me that for two days, and I don't remember anything about it. That was our experience of going to New York the first time.

I always loved New York, not for any reason other than I always was pretty lucky. I won the Garden rodeo nine or ten times in the twelve years that I went there. It was always a pretty good place for me.

What did you do during the daytime?

Most of the time you just rodeoed. Sharon went to a few plays. I didn't go to many. I always felt like if you watched the stock or the guys you might learn something that would help you. My theory was that I was in the rodeo business. A lot of guys would go to a picture show. I went to the rodeo. I'd work during a performance from opening the gates to running the chutes. Every little bit helped to try to pay the bills and raise them kids.

Jim, I know you. The longer you watched the stock, the better chance you had to know what the stock was going to do when you got on it.

That was my theory. It didn't hurt to watch them. I just thought that was the way I was trying to make a living, I ought to try to do it a little harder.

In New York I just rode bareback broncs and bulls. In those days you got more bucking horses than you did bareback horses or bulls. So I could make more rodeos by working two events.

I'd ride broncs a lot in the summer when I was going to a particular rodeo. The saddle bronc riding was a fun event for me, but I was pretty well able to make a living riding bareback horses and bulls and going to a lot more rodeos that way. I even placed in the calf roping a time or two. But primarily, the bull riding and the bronc riding was what I did to make a living.

Over fifty years ago, a jeans company introduced a new product to the rodeo world, and I know that you've been associated with them for quite a while. How long have you been associated with Wrangler?

I've really been associated with them since 1947. They came to Madison Square Garden in 1947, which was the first year I was there. They brought a semi load of jeans and snap-button shirts and jackets. They gave every contestant two pair of jeans and shirts and hired some of them to endorse their product.

Levi was their biggest competitor and Lee was next. I was just a kid a year out of high school, so they didn't think anything about me. But I lucked out and won New York that fall in both events, so the next spring in Denver they asked me if I would like to be an endorsee. It paid $150 just to have them take your picture, so I said, "You bet."

I went to work for them in 1948 and have been with them for over fifty years. I tell people I've never worn out a pair of Wranglers, but I've outgrown a few.

I've also been associated with Justin Boot Company since 1949. I've never been around anyone who enjoyed people more than John and Jane Justin. They were my special friends.

I want you to tell us about the bull, Tornado. That song I wrote about Freckles Brown riding him opened the door for me to get involved in the world of rodeo as an entertainer. Some of the best friends I'll ever have I got in the world of rodeo, and I owe all of it to that song. Tornado is buried at the Hall of Fame in Oklahoma City. Tell us about that bull.

A good friend, John Williams, bought Tornado with some other bulls at a sale barn. He sent him to us in Mesquite and we bucked him three or four times. The first big rodeo I took him to was in Memphis, Tennessee. I was still riding bulls and producing rodeos, and I thought I'd like to ride him after seeing him buck.

The next year we took him to every rodeo, and he really bucked and everyone went to talking about him. When Freckles had him at the finals, they figured out he'd been out over two hundred times. We got an awful lot of publicity about him. I knew someday somebody was going to ride him, and I was afraid it would be some kid just starting out. But it was really great that Freckles rode him when he did and where he did. You couldn't have staged it any better for a movie.

I also had a bull called Mighty Mouse that went three or four years without a qualified ride on him. My son Marvin Paul drew him at the National Finals in '73, and he rode him for the first time. That was really the year that tickled me.

I want to just turn you loose and let you tell us stories about interesting things that have happened to you and things that you've seen.

I've made more good friends in the rodeo business than anybody, I guess. You can't hardly talk about rodeo to very many people without coming up with a Casey Tibbs story. He was from South Dakota, where you didn't have to have a driver's license, and he always drove fast.

One time he was out in Arizona, and a cop stopped him for speeding. Casey told the cop he was the world's champion bronc rider and was running late for a rodeo. He said the cop could just look at his belt buckle if he didn't believe him. The cop said, "Are you really THE Casey Tibbs?"

And when he said "Yes," the cop said, "I'm really glad to see you. We've got a warrant out for your arrest!" It cost him something like $300, and they hauled him off to jail.

I've got a memory bank full of good stories, some about Damon Bond, a real cowboy and rancher from New Mexico. He ran our ranch and pretty near raised my kids while I was out rodeoing.

We had an old Studebaker truck, and one winter we were going to get a load of cake out of a box car. A blue norther hit, and it was really cold. We kept a six-gallon keg of moonshine to winter on, so I got a fruit jar and filled it for the trip.

Coming back I said I thought next time I would get a fifth-size bottle so it would be easier to hold. Damon just shook his head and said, "If it was any easier to drink, wouldn't either one of us be able to drive that truck!"

What kind of guy was Bill Linderman?
King was what everybody called Bill. He was big, tough, domineering, and intimidating, but he was also a nice guy. If the water got rough, it was nice to have Bill on your team. He was a fair guy, and he really helped the rodeo association.

The world knows that you are the winningest cowboy in history. How many world champion buckles do you have?
I have sixteen of them altogether. One night Harry Tompkins was making an after-dinner speech at a school, and the president introduced him. He didn't say he was an eight-time world champion. Instead, he said, "I'm the guy who kept Jim Shoulders from winning twenty-two world championships." That was true. I was runner-up to him six times.

Harry was the closest friend I had for a long time in the rodeo business. He loaned me money for a down payment on my first house.

Jim, you are a tremendous asset to the sport and to your community. You're a lucky man, and rodeo is lucky you came along.
Yes, I've been very fortunate in rodeo. That's always been my story—I'd rather be lucky than smart.

(Interviewed in 1998)

JOHN GAITHER

John Gaither is probably, at seventy-five plus, America's oldest living, working cowboy. John works horseback every day. He is as good a cowboy as ever came down the pike. He is an outstanding hand with horses, and he understands cattle better than the cattle do. It has been a great thrill for me to spend lots of mornings "Waitin' on the Drive" with John. He is very spiritual. He loves the Lord more than anything else and is faithful to his teachings. He is a wonderful inspiration to all who know him.

I remember one morning on the rim of Croton Canyon out on the Four Sixes when John and I were quietly admiring the morning and listening to the drive come together. John said to me, "If a man can sit out here this morning and tell me there's no such thing as a God, he sure needs to be someplace else." That was the beginning of my album, Faith and Values. *John is my special friend, and I am so proud that he is a big part of my life.*

John, tell us a little bit about where you grew up.

I was born in Monument, New Mexico, and went to school in different places. When I was born, my mother's milk wasn't any good. Carnation or Eagle Brand wouldn't work either, so an old XIT cowboy milked a jenny —a female burro — and brought the milk over. And another man milked a mare and brought that milk over. In about a month I got straightened out. My wife says that's the reason I'm so stubborn.

I worked for Jim Cooper for a while and kind of learned to break horses with him and his son. Then I got a job breaking horses on a

John Gaither

ranch near Judkins. That was in '36, so you know how tough it was to get a job.

My folks split up and I stayed with my grandmother until I was four, and then I stayed with my aunt and went to school in Amarillo and then Lovington. I first started school at Pearl, west of

Monument. Everybody rode horses to school. We only had one doctor in the whole county, and he came out there to die. He cured himself of tuberculosis and lived to be ninety-seven years old.

I went to work for the Diamond A's that was on nine hundred sections. A guy named Clabe Kyle ran that outfit. He was a great cowboy. He and Tom Ross, the outlaw that killed a cattle inspector, had some good horses. At that time the government was furnishing stallions—racehorses that broke down on the track. As long as you took care of them, you could keep them. If the stall was bad or anything, they were gone. They'd also buy horses for the cavalry—I was really thrilled to get rid of some of them.

I rode some broncs, but not all the time. I mostly was with a cow outfit, and I broke a few horses in the wintertime. I remember the blizzard when a lot of cattle froze to death. They came from the XIT and the LSD, west of Lubbock. They wound up down by Jal. They had a bunch of wagons down there and sorted those cattle for days. About the only thing they could do with those dead cattle was to skin 'em and get their hides.

Tell me about some of the big outfits you worked for.

Well, there was the Waggoners and the Diamond A's, but the greatest was the Four Sixes. I went there in '72 as a welding man.

And when did you start rodeoing?

About '36. I didn't ride all the time, just every once in a while. Pretty soon I could ride bulls.

The worst horse I ever rode was named Rattler at the Diamond A. He was bad news for anybody. The old boy who broke him was a good bronc rider. I wanted to ride him, and the first time I got on him, he throwed me. When I hit the ground, I rolled under the fence, and he hit the fence right behind me. We couldn't get him to stand up, so they put a rope around his neck, and I fixed a mule to a wagon to pull him. He finally came up, and we circled around and around him. We drove him into the barn and he knocked a hole in the barn. I rode him all winter, but that was the most miserable winter I ever spent in my life. That was worse than the war.

***Let's talk a little bit more about the Sixes. Things haven't
changed much since '72, have they?***

It's still a good place to work. Of all the places I've ever worked, I
don't have any real bad memories of any of them.

The wagon still went out when you were at the Sixes, didn't it?

Yeah, we used to camp at the Taylor Camp.

***Let's take one pasture, the South Ash. That's some of the most
dramatic country in West Texas. It's about fifteen or sixteen
thousand acres. How long would you stay in that pasture?***

Sometimes we'd make two or three drives in there. We'd try to get
it in one drive, but we'd hardly ever get it clean. When you're coming
out of those canyons, there's so many things that can happen. Lot of
times, we have to make two drives.

***I grew up in cow country and thinking I wanted to be a cowboy. But
I never did really make my living as a cowboy. When I first started
going to the Sixes about '74 or '75, I remember lots of times you and
some others would watch out for me. I remember the first time J.J.
had me drag calves, you fixed my rope on my saddle so I wouldn't
get hurt. You guys were real important in my life and still are.***

You know your singing was the highlight. That helps your whole
attitude in life. Turn off the radio and TV. We can entertain ourselves.

***Going out in that wagon and sleeping out there, spending the
early evening hours with the guys, swapping stories, those are the
times that will forever be precious to me. I really think those times
changed my life and gave me an appreciation for things I didn't
have before. I try to impress on people that the cowboy is not a
hard-ridin', gun-totin', cussin' kind of character. He is a
God-loving, dedicated family man. He's all the things people
would like to be themselves and want their neighbor to be.***

You know, when you're working for somebody, if they want it
upside down and backward, it's all right with me. If I'm drawing their
wages, I think they've got a right to tell me how they want it done. If

I'm not happy somewhere, I won't gripe and groan about it. I'll go somewhere else and not make everybody else miserable.

It's a shame our society has digressed from that. It took us a long time to get there, but it hasn't taken long to digress from it. Now, John you finished up at the Sixes. You retired at the Sixes in 1991, after nineteen years. That was the longest you ever worked one ranch. What's the reason cowboys move around so much — is it because they want to see new country?

I was really more content at the Sixes than I was at any place else. I took care of the mares and colts and the studs until Doc came along, and then I worked for him. I like the mares and little colts. You know horses aren't a sideline to me—it's a way of life. Of course, cowboying is, too.

I've seen you flank calves when you were in your mid-seventies, and I've seen you out-work two twenty-five-year-old men.

Well, I've been fortunate to have good health. Just like now. I'm still doing day work. Cowboying is a fatal disease. Once you get stung by that bug you'll never get over it. Some of your songs talk about old-time cowboys that was fixin' to cross the great divide, so to speak.

John, why do you think we like to live in the past?

You don't want to dwell in the past. When you have a tragedy in your family, you can't let it get you down. You've got to bow your neck and go on. Cowboying is a lot like that. I just never was one to bother people with my troubles. Most of the time you make them bigger when you involve other people.

In the early days when you went to the Sixes, it was still pretty brushy. I remember in the late '70s, they cleared the mesquites. It made world of difference.

Those old cows that was used to getting away, they'd get out in the open and throw their old head up looking for some brush, and there wasn't any brush. They don't know what to do.

***I've been wanting you to tell me a story about the sheriff
of Lea County, New Mexico.***

This guy named Bilbrey was the sheriff. He got elected sheriff because the women were tired of bootleggers. There was a fellow who lived over there between Hobbs and the Texas line, and he was a deacon in the Baptist Church. When Bilbrey rode up on him, he was cookin' up his mash. Bilbrey told him he was going to have to take him in because he was duty-bound to take in the bootleggers. The Baptist deacon agreed he had sinned and asked the sheriff to go over by a windmill and pray for him. After about 30 minutes, they went back to get the still, and this old boy's son had moved it across the state line. So, I guess the Lord answered his prayers.

Now, let me tell you about this lady named Willie Evans. She got pneumonia like a lot of people in those days. Her father-in-law, her daddy, and her son all got it and died. And she had triplets, all within three weeks. She raised those kids by driving a school bus. Neighbors would take her stuff and help her.

***Those were good days and good people. We like to live in the past
and dream about the past, but the good old days are right now.***

That's right, and you know we have a great future if we just latch onto it.

(Interviewed in 1996)

RICHARD FARNSWORTH

Richard was one of the greatest actors of all time. He was also one of the finest human beings who ever graced the screen, the rodeo arena, or the whole of America. He was as unassuming as a person can be yet extremely confident in his talent and his ability to accomplish almost anything he tried. His role in The Grey Fox *will be remembered as one of the great character roles of all time.*

I was very fortunate that Richard was my good friend, and as I look out in my pasture, I am reminded of him every day; his old gray horse, Foxy, grazes just outside my window.

Richard loved New Mexico and his home in Lincoln was always open to anyone who wanted to talk about the West and especially about cowboys. We all miss Richard, but he left us a lot to hang onto and to remember him by. As I said at his memorial service, "He left a good string of horses on this side of the river. They are honesty, integrity, loyalty, work ethic, common decency, and respect." I thank you, Richard.

On Cowboy Corner, we talked about his early days.

My great-grandfather, John D. Culver, came to Los Angeles in 1882 and built some of the first waterworks there. He later got to be an engineer and built the LA aqueduct in 1920 and 1921.

Harry Culver was a great-uncle of mine and he established Culver City, California. I grew up in Southern California in the San Fernando Valley. I went to junior high school for about a year and quit in 1935 during the Depression. I went to work around the barns mucking out stalls.

Richard Farnsworth

Were these polo horses or just horses that people were boarding?

These were just privately owned horses. But, we had a celebrity polo team that consisted of Will Rogers, Walt Disney, Spencer Tracy, and Darryl Zanuck. When Argentina guys would come up, our guys would just wax 'em. Those guys were really good horsemen. Will Rogers had a little polo field of his own in Santa Monica Canyon in 1934. I was fourteen years old and I'd gather up horses. Will would give you fifty cents, and the rest of the guys would give you a quarter. You'd make two or three dollars a day. A lot of grown men were working for a dollar a day then.

Richard Farnsworth and Red

You told me one time you met Will James.

Yeah, I met Will James in 1934. They were making a movie called *Smoky the Cow Horse*. Fat Jones, who later became Ben Johnson's father-in-law, was supplying the stock. Will James had envisioned a horse that was grulla-colored. They were having trouble finding a horse that matched the color, and in those days, they didn't paint horses. They needed horses that would buck, rear up, fall down.

They had a black horse at Fat Jones Stable that had done a lot of pictures. He was called Rex, the King of the Wild Horses. Victor Jory, who was gonna ride the horse in the movie, had been taking lessons on the black horse and really liked him. So they called Fox Studios and had Will James come out to Fat Jones Stable.

Will said, "I don't care what you got, I'm going to have a grulla play the part of Smokey." Fat said, "Take a look at the black horse first." Swede Lindell was the trainer. Now this old horse would fight you. Swede stepped over into the pen, the old horse rushed him, Swede jumped across the fence and the old horse came to a sliding stop, reached up with his teeth, and ripped the top board off the fence. Will James said, "By God, that's Cougar," which was the name of the horse in the film.

Tell me about the Cowboy Turtles Association that later became the Professional Rodeo Cowboys Association.

Well, it revolutionized the rodeo business as far as the contestants were concerned. They organized in 1937, and got it to where the promoter had to put up a bond before the contestants would work. That worked fine, and the prize money got better. I joined in '41. Four of us had an old 1937 pickup truck and drove to Chicago. They asked me for my Turtle card, and I said I didn't have one because I was an amateur. It cost $10 to join, which I did. It was the best thing I ever did. You were guaranteed whatever the program said you were guaranteed. I rode bulls, and I tried to bulldog a little if the steers weren't too big. I only weighed about 140 pounds.

Tell us about the time you came to Fort Worth. That was an interesting time.

I had been to Chicago and didn't do any good there. A fellow named Johnny Curtis said if I went to Fort Worth with him, he would get me one of the best jobs in town. I went to work at a mule barn in 1941. It paid two dollars a day. The government had thousands of two and three-year-old colts shipped in. It was awful tough work. I stayed there a couple of months and then I had to go back to California to rodeo some more.

I had saved $7, and a ticket on a Greyhound bus cost $18 to Los Angeles. They told me about Benny Binion and said he might help me out. I found him and told him my story. He loaned me $20 so I'd have a little eating money on the way back. Years later, Ben Johnson and I were at his place in Las Vegas, and I reminded him about the loan. He didn't remember it, but I told him I wanted to pay him back. He said, "No, just go put it on a hard eight out on the crap table."

After you got back to California, did you go back to mucking stalls right away?

No, I had done a little bit of picture work since 1937. So I went back and got a couple of fairly good jobs doing some stunts. I rodeoed for another six or seven years and finally I started a family and quit rodeoing in 1950. By that time I was doing very well as a stuntman.

I was mucking out stalls at the polo barn in 1937. A couple of guys drove up one day from Paramount Pictures and asked me if I knew where there were any ponies that looked like a Mongolian horse, and I said I knew of a couple.

They said if I knew anybody who rode a little, they were going to do a couple of weeks' worth of work north of Los Angeles. I asked what it paid. He said it was $7 a day and a box lunch. I said that sounded good. So I asked the boss if he could spare me for a couple of weeks. He said, "Oh, heck, we won't have any trouble there. You're fired."

I went up and did the picture. That $7 a day up against $5 a week looked pretty good, and I've stayed in the picture business off and on ever since.

I found out early in my career I wasn't accident prone. I was light, and I could hit the ground pretty hard and get up and walk away. I also doubled just about everybody who was anywhere near my size. I was six feet and weighed about 145 pounds. I doubled guys like Hank Fonda, Guy Madison, Rory Calhoun, and Joel McCrea. I doubled Montgomery Clift in *Red River*. We were about the same size.

You told me a story about a stunt you were going to do with a lion one time.

Republic Studios called and wanted a man to double the old black comedian named Stepin Fetchit. The shot had a tree with a seven-foot limb in it, and they wanted me to run and jump up and catch it and sit in the tree. Then they were going to turn an old MGM lion loose. He had been declawed and didn't have any teeth, so I didn't think anything about it. Then they were going to put Stepin Fetchit up there and get a shot of him shaking and scared to death.

I asked them about the money. They said they had $200 in the budget, so if they had to do it more than once, that's all I would get paid. I didn't see any problem. But the old lion they were supposed to use wasn't feeling good, so they had to bring out two others. One was real aggressive and had left claw marks above the tree limb I was supposed to jump up and catch. I had a premonition about it, and I decided not to do the stunt. Somebody did it, and the picture was released. But my intuition has helped me in a lot of cases when things didn't look right.

Tell us about your first speaking part.

I was doing some stunts in a Roy Rogers pictures, and Gabby Hayes was his sidekick then. They had Gabby Hayes and a little boy trapped down in a canyon in a cabin. The outlaws were shooting into the cabin trying to flush him out. They had the camera on me and another fellow. He and I were really tough, killing people, blowing up bridges and banks.

In the story, we finally got old Gabby cornered down in the canyon. They had a thing called a squib that looks like bullets hitting behind you. A guy stood behind the camera with a slingshot and could put it anywhere he wanted. So in the story I was supposed to get a couple of shots close to my head and say, "This is more than I bargained for, Slade, I'm pulling out."

The situation struck me so funny—we were supposed to be the toughest men in the West, and all we took was a couple of shots. They rolled the camera, and I couldn't get through it. I started to laugh. We tried it two more times, and the last time was the worst. I just fell apart. So they got another man, and he did a hell of a good job.

There was one particular movie that made a lot of difference in your life. Tell us about that movie and what it meant to you.

The first recognizable part I ever did was in 1976 on a film called *The Duchess and the Dirtwater Fox.* I was hired as a stagecoach driver. The director asked me if I had ever thought about trying to make it as an actor. I said I had tried it and didn't think I could cut it.

But about a year later I got a call to go on a picture called *Comes a Horseman*. I had a little more confidence, so I read a few lines. I thought it was too much, but the director told me to take it home and look at it. My wife looked at it and said I could do it. I read a few lines to the director, and he said that would be fine, to just leave it that way and it would be fine. So we shot it, and everything worked out fine. In fact, I was nominated for a supporting actor that year. So from then on, I just did parts that I could handle.

Did you work for John Ford?

Yeah, I did seven or eight films for him. He was the stuntman's idol. There was always a lot of action, and you made a lot of money.

I think the last one I did was *Cheyenne Autumn*. The first one was *Fort Apache* with James Stewart and John Wayne. That was in 1947.

He was hard on actors. If a stuntman made a mistake, it was an honest mistake. But when an actor blew his lines, there was no excuses for it. He got the job done with them. I would say he was pretty opinionated.

There were a lot of wonderful people who worked for John Ford, and one of them was a very dear friend of yours and mine, Ben Johnson.

Yeah, I met Ben when he came out to California with a load of horses for Howard Hughes to make *The Outlaw*. Ben was always a down-to-earth good person. He had a lot of fine qualities about him that a lot of actors lost when they got in the business and did well for a while. He was always a friend of the working man.

Another great one was Gene Autry. He made a tremendous contribution to the movie world, but he also made the biggest contribution to the music business of his time. The musical legacy he left for us will never be duplicated.

You're sure right. He came at a time when people were needing a good, honest person they could believe. And that was his claim to fame. He's my idol.

***Let's talk about* The Grey Fox. *That movie probably did you
more good than any you've ever done.***

I think it did, and it was probably the easiest thing I've ever done
in my life. The dialogue flowed so smooth, and I kind of identified
with that old man. He was in the paperbacks I read in the '30s, Bill
Miner the train robber. Here he was, this old man with gray hair and
a white mustache. Sixty years later, I grew into looking kind of like
him, and I portrayed his life story. I got the Canadian Oscar for that.
I also won a Canadian award for *Anne of Green Gables* and an academy nomination for *Comes a Horseman.*

***You did a show with Wilford Brimley, one of the greatest actors
of our time. Let's talk a little bit about* The Natural *and
what it was like to work with Wilford.***

It was great to work with him. I had known him for years. He had
a look about him that was different. The funny part of *The Natural*
was that neither one of us had ever hit a baseball in our lives. The
director, Barry Levinson, didn't care, and it worked out fine.

What are you doing with your life today?

I'm not doing a heck of a lot, but I've got this little place out in
Lincoln, New Mexico. I've got just enough stock to get up in the
morning, throw something to them, fix a little fence, and then go
watch TV all day, which is the type of work I'm cut out for.

***I was with you in Oklahoma City at the Cowboy Hall of Fame
when you were inducted into the Hall of Great Western
Performers. That's a tremendous honor to be selected
to spend eternity in the Cowboy Hall of Fame.***

Red, I still kind of think somebody else could have got it. But if
they want to give it to me, I'll darn sure take it.

(Interviewed in 1996)

ROY CLARK

Roy Clark not only is one of my closest friends but one of my favorite people in the whole world. Roy and I have known each other since the late 1950's. I think that he is one of the most talented people who ever graced the stage. He is a master musician, a powerful singer, and one of the most entertaining personalities show business has ever known.

Having known him for all these years, I know that Roy has a tremendous interest in the Western way of life and especially horses. With that knowledge and forty years of experiences together, this was an especially rewarding interview for me. Roy's contribution to the world of television and country music is immeasurable. The legacy that he has created already will live forever. And he ain't near through!

Even though I knew the answer, I asked Roy about where he was born and raised.

I was born in a very rural section of Virginia. There is absolutely nothing there as far as work. The only industry is logging. I got in on a little bit of all of that as a kid. I went back in the woods with them with mule teams and logging wagons. I've always thought I was blessed that I saw that. One of my chores was to churn milk to make butter—just the real basic stuff. I feel sorry for the kids who have never known that part of life.

How'd you start playing guitar?

My dad and his brothers played for what they called house dances. They'd move the furniture out and roll up the carpet. They'd

Roy Clark

put the instruments on their shoulders in a pillowcase and walk around and play for people who lived out in the country. They'd stand out in the yard and play, and the lady of the house would give them a glass of lemonade, and then they'd go on to the next house.

That was a little bit before I came along, but I was raised around music. I picked around on the banjo and the mandolin a little bit, but it wasn't until I was thirteen years old and a neighbor had a guitar that he let me try. I strummed my fingers down that thing and it was like a light switch. I just said, "I want to learn to play." For that Christmas I got a guitar from Sears and two books, *300 Chords for Guitar and How to Use Them* and a book of favorite songs and how to become extremely popular and invited out on Saturday nights a lot.

And the caption to that is, a lady came to me last year, the widow of the man who had that guitar, and gave it to me. It was the first guitar I ever touched, not the first I learned to play. I would have recognized it in a room full of five hundred guitars. When I saw that guitar, my life just flashed before my eyes.

You know Roy, that's how Bob Wills got started.

Bob Wills told me a story one time. He played a fiddle because it was the only instrument left. They brought in a fellow who was a music teacher and specialized in violin. After about a week, this fellow went to Bob's daddy and said he didn't think he was going to teach this young fellow anything. But he said he wouldn't mess with him because Bob was going to be able to find something of his own that was going to be special. This guy had the intelligence to not mess with something coming out from inside.

If you'll remember, I saw you in Amarillo, Texas, at the Continental Club in 1958.

You know that's something I've been thinking about recently—those show dances. We'd do maybe three shows a night, and in between that we'd play and they would dance. When you're doing a show, you're creating and performing. But when you play the dance part, you almost become a part of the audience. I really miss that. There used to be dance halls all over this country.

I was playing around Washington, D.C. I had done local radio and television and all the clubs and was pretty well known in about a three-hundred-mile radius. I asked myself if I wanted to keep doing that or try to build a career with some security. About that time

Wanda Jackson came to Washington. She said she was getting ready to go to Las Vegas to headline at the Golden Nugget and she needed someone to open the show. That's how I made a move. I met Wanda's manager in Las Vegas, and he said he thought I had a great future and wanted to be a part of it. Things started to fall in place, and I was asked to sign with Capitol Records.

Is that when Joe Allison started working with you as a producer?

Yes. Ken Nelson came to me when Wanda and I were doing a record in Nashville. He signed me as an instrumentalist and said they would work me in as a singer a little bit at a time. Wanda told Joe about me because she said I could really sell a song.

So Joe played me a song, *Tips of My Fingers,* that was on the other side of a Bill Anderson record. He got Hank Levine to write a big arrangement for it. The day we were going to record, all these musicians started filing in—all the cellos and violins. I think there was a harp and six vocalists. We thought we were in the wrong studio. We recorded it the first time without a stop, so the first thing Ken Nelson heard was the complete song, top to bottom, full bore.

He came out and put his arm around my neck and said, "I have to tell you, I thought we were in serious trouble. But don't worry about it—it's a hit."

Did you do Yesterday When I Was Young *in that same session?*

Oh, no. *Tips of My Fingers* was like 1963. *Yesterday When I Was Young* didn't come along until about 1970.

Roy, after all those years in Las Vegas you still do Las Vegas and you still travel. Do you remember any really funny stories from when you were on the road?

We were traveling in a six-year-old Cadillac pulling a plywood trailer with our instruments in it. We were driving to Independence, Kansas, from Las Vegas and were on a narrow road when someone tried to pass me. I wondered what kind of idiot would do that. Then I looked and saw some sparks, and I said, "That's our trailer!" The tongue of it was pounding in the concrete. Then the trailer flipped over and busted like a pumpkin. Everything was busted for about a quarter of a mile. It wasn't very funny at the time.

My guitar was busted. And there were no speakers left in the amplifier. Hank Thompson had just traded his in to a guy in Independence, Kansas. So we got that, and I salvaged my guitar.

Speaking of Hank Thompson, tell the folks about going antelope hunting with him in Wyoming.

This was really funny. We used to go up to Medicine Bow. I knew a lady who owned the Virginian Hotel and that was our headquarters. I always got the Owen Wister suite where he wrote *The Virginian*. We wanted trophies. We weren't just out there to slaughter the antelope herd.

We were back at the hotel that evening, and our guide said he knew where the big bucks were. They were on someone's spread, and he wouldn't let people hunt. We asked him to ask the man if we could hunt, so he went out there to talk to him. So he told the man he had Hank Thompson and Roy Clark and Roy Clark's dad who wanted to hunt trophy antelope on his place.

He finally said, "Well, I guess that'd be all right, but I don't want to make a habit of that." The guide thanked him and started to leave when the man stopped him and said, "Next time you come out here, see if you can bring Lawrence Welk."

You told me a story about how you and your daddy went up to see one of your uncles in the mountains.

Dad hadn't seen his uncle in Lord knows how many years. He knew about where he lived, so I suggested we go out and visit him. So we went out, and we asked directions. They pointed to a hill and said he lived on the back side of it, but the road didn't go up there. They said to just drive until we ran out of road, so we did.

Then we started walking on a trail and came to a creek. It was pretty fast-moving but not too deep, so we waded across it. The trail kept getting more narrow. Finally we came to a mule tied to a tree. It seemed to me the only reason that mule was there was to ride on up the trail.

So my dad and I got on that mule and rode to where we finally could see the shape of a building that was a little old shanty. We got off the mule and walked up on the porch. We hollered and didn't hear anything, but we saw a note on the screen door. It said, "Sorry I missed you. I've gone to the country to fish." I thought, Lord, if this isn't the country, where did he go?

I know you have a tremendous love of horses and keep horses on your place up in northeastern Oklahoma.

Horses have been a big part of my life. I used to ride work horses and mules. I remember when they used to bring movies into the little town I was born in. My cousin and I would always act out what we'd seen at the movie. Gene Autry came out, and boy that was it—the music that was inside of me.

My cousin used to ride me about it. He'd say, "He ain't no cowboy—he's a singer." But we'd ride milk cows and whatever came along, and I carried that with me as I grew up.

A friend of mine had a horse I got on. His German Shepherd was barking and the horse was raring up and stuff. The dog got underneath the horse where he couldn't see him, and instead of giving him his head, I pulled back on him. He had a Mexican bit in his mouth, and the harder I pulled, the more he came back. He fell and came down across my leg, and I didn't walk for eleven months. But I never blamed the horse.

Then I got into thoroughbred racehorses, and one thing led to another. I gave one to my wife, Barbara, for Christmas and it became the foundation mare for our operation. There's nothing like helping with the delivery of a foal and seeing it stand up and nurse and then kicking up and down. Then seeing it in training and starting to race with your colors on it—there's just nothing like it.

Barbara's mare got a bone chip in her front leg, and we decided to have it operated on. The doctors removed it, and she healed. But later it started hurting her again, and we let her out to be a brood mare.

Back then Barbara had real long fingernails, and it just used to irritate me because she couldn't even get a key in the door. So one day we were going riding, and I told her I wasn't going to saddle her horse. So I looked, and I saw her nails were trimmed way back. I'd been after her for two years, and I asked why she all of a sudden trimmed them. She said it was because she couldn't saddle her horse. She wouldn't do it for me, but she did it for a horse.

What kind of horses do you have today and what are you doing musically?

We have mostly thoroughbreds, a couple of quarter horses and a couple of Appaloosas. I got into Appaloosa horses because my riding horse was an Appaloosa. I bought a mare in Kansas, and she was a tiny little thing. Everybody called her Mighty Mouse. She was the best race horse I ever had—she never let you down. She just had a foal, and the next morning she was laying in the stall dead. I guess of all the horses I had, that was the most personal loss.

Musically, I still have a big band, and we're probably out on the road about two hundred days a year.

(Interviewed in 2001)

JOHN JUSTIN

There will never be another man as influential in his chosen profession as was John Justin in the Western footwear industry. John and his family not only were innovative, but their marketing skills were geared to the public who either wears cowboy boots on a daily basis or dreams of being a cowboy. The name Justin Boots is synonymous throughout the world with excellence in finish, fit, and style.

One of the proudest treasures of my life was the friendship of John and Jane Justin. I miss them greatly. It was a great pleasure to visit with John about his background and the industry that he capitalized was created by his grandfather, H.J. Justin. He started out this way:

My father's father came from Lafayette, Indiana, down to this part of the country. He got down as far as Spanish Fort, Texas, up on the Red River. To get enough money to eat on, he got a job in the barber shop.

Some fellow came along who had torn his boot. He asked if my grandfather could fix the boot, and he said he could. So he stitched it up, and that guy told somebody else about him. Finally, someone came along and asked my grandfather if he could make him a pair of boots, and he said, "If you'll get me the leather, I can." He made that pair and then another pair.

The trail herds came through Spanish Fort on their way to Dodge City. His boots went up the trail with the cowboys. Guys in Dodge

City would draw an outline of their feet and send it back down the trail to have boots made.

Later the railroad came through there and established the town of Nocona, which is named after a chief of the Comanche Indians. That's where I was born, and they started making boots there. They started in a shed and then built what was a modern factory. One of their first customers was a firm in Fort Worth. They would take your orders, draw the outline of your foot and send it to Nocona. In those days, they got $10 for the boot and a dollar for the dealer.

How was that boot different from the boot the average person wears today?

It was a lot heavier and was made for being out in the dirt and riding horseback. There was an old leather they used called a French wax calf that was calfskin stuffed with a lot of tallow to make them good and heavy and substantial.

The toe was more rounded then because they wanted them roomy. They wanted a real serviceable boot, and they started stitching some pattern on the top to give the top a little more stability. Then they started to sell more and put inlays in them and fancy stitching and things like that.

Was the high heel a part of the original boot?

Well the old story was that the high heel was there so your foot wouldn't slip through the stirrup, and you had something to push your foot against. And, also, if you wanted to saddle your horse in the morning and he was a little frisky, you could put your heels in the ground and stop him from sliding too much. The shank, right underneath your foot in the middle, and the heel were very important. They would take spikes or heavy nails and flatten them out for the shank. That would give them a platform to stand on.

How long did the company stay in Nocona?

I don't know exactly what year they moved there. It was in the late 1800s. Then they started to do more business and sell through dealers. So they decided they needed a bigger town with more trans-

John Justin

portation in different directions. Everybody got after the Justins to move to Waco and Dallas and Fort Worth and Abilene. They finally decided Fort Worth was the place to go because they had the packing houses and it was known as where the West begins.

At the time my aunt, my father's sister, didn't want to move and tried to discourage them from moving. She stayed until she was the only one left up there. In the meantime, she had ordered some equipment and started the Nocona Boot Co. Of course, it was a family situation then—some of it went pretty good, and some of it went pretty bad. She did a good job of running it. Finally we bought it, and it's a part of our organization now.

Explain the " last" and why some boots fit some people's feet and some don't.

Well, they started the last many years ago. The last is the form over which the leather is stretched to define the size and shape of the boot. In the old days, shoemaking was a localized deal, and you just got something that sort of fit you. Really what got sizes and widths into the deal was the Civil War. They knew they'd lose half their soldiers on the way because they would get blisters on their feet. So they got the quartermaster to get the last made that approximated the human foot.

The lasts in those days were expensive and hard to come by. So you'd use your last for a lot of people. Then they started making more standard lasts with widths and lengths. Everybody made them a little different for a while. The old saying is, "The last comes first."

How many pair of boots did your grandfather make in a week?

I'd say he would make six or eight pair a week. Now we make several thousand. We've been up as high as ten thousand a week. The shoemaking machinery came along, but bootmaking was a fringe on that. Not much attention was paid to them, and you did by hand what you didn't have the equipment to do. There was an old rattle-trap machine that was used to do the stitching around the top and to put the pull-straps on and things like that.

Who are the people who wear your boots?

The core business is people who work in feedlots or drive trucks. Some people wear them in the city. Doctors wear them a lot because they're on their feet so much, and boots will keep your feet in good shape. Most of our sales are in the Southwest, but we sell more up in the East than we used to.

Where do the leathers come from?

They used to be tanned domestically. But the laws on pollution now are such that there are very few tanneries left in this country. We get a lot from South America. And, of course you get a lot of the exotics like ostrich from Africa.

When did you get in the boot business?

I really got into it in the early '50s. I tried to get into it when I was younger, but my father and his two brothers didn't have room for anybody else in there. So I started a belt company with a fine gentleman named W.D. Barton, and I did better than I ever thought I would do. In the early '50s, they began to see they had to have someone in there, so I came in and started working in the boot factory. I've been at it ever since and loving every minute of it. Right now I'm just really unhappy I can't get in the factory and make boots myself.

Tell us about your early life and the things that prepared you for a career in the boot business.

I was born in Nocona and came to Fort Worth when I was seven years old. I went to school in Fort Worth and then went to Washington, D.C., and graduated from high school there. I did a little bit of everything there. I was a messenger, and I thought it was great. I finally was transferred to Dallas in the National Recovery Administration under President Roosevelt.

I worked there a while and then decided I should quit and get more education. I went my first year at Oklahoma A&M at Stillwater and then came back and went to TCU. But I was making belts all night and going to school in the day, and it was killing me. So I finally had to quit school.

How many years have you been the chairman of the board for the Southwestern Exposition and Livestock Show?

I don't know, eight or ten years or maybe longer than that. From '61 to '63 I was the mayor of Fort Worth.

***You told me one time that everybody in town had your
phone number while you were mayor.***

Yes, the door was always open. People would call me about traffic lights, chug holes, and any other kind of problem that the citizens were having. They always called me in the middle of the night and they'd say, "I wanted to call you now because I knew you weren't busy."

***You have always had an open door policy at your company,
also, and I personally know a large number of your employees.
Every single one of them respects the fact that they can talk to you
about a problem. John, that builds tremendous loyalty.
When did you take over the boot company?***

I took over the boot company around 1950. I had started the belt company in 1938 and was working at the boot company at that time, but I had just a menial job.

***Fort Worth is your home and very special to you. What are the
things that are important to you to preserve Fort Worth?***

I think our Western heritage is so important because that's what we have that very few other people have. We've got this great equestrian center over here. I go by it every day and there are trailers there every day. I think the Western heritage is what we've really got to protect. We have to really fight to keep it.

(Interviewed in 1999)

WILFORD BRIMLEY

When I measure my friends by how much I care for them, how much I admire and respect them, plus all the things that we have in common, Wilford Brimley is at the top of my list. He is one of the most wholesome, genuine people I have ever known. His heart is as big as all outdoors and he'll cry at a Kentucky Fried Chicken opening. His emotions are the primary factor that makes him one of the greatest actors the world will ever know.

He's a cowman, a horseman, a great father, a better grandfather, a good husband and as close a friend as this cowboy will ever have. I enjoy his company very much and was very proud when he consented to do an interview for Cowboy Corner.

Wilford has a very interesting history and heritage in the great state of Utah. When I asked him about that, this is how he replied:

My heritage is very important to me. I'm a product of the Rocky Mountain West. My grandfather came from Wales when he was ten years old. He walked from Omaha to Salt Lake Valley pulling a wagon with his clothes in it. My mother's people came from Star Valley, Wyoming. They're Danish, so I would be a Danish-Welsh cross pretty much.

I left home when I was quite young and went a lot of places. I did a lot of things and met a lot of people, and I'm grateful for the opportunities this America has afforded me.

My dad was a trader—he bought and sold anything that ate. Chickens, geese, ducks, cows, horses, whatever. I inherited from him an affinity for four-legged animals.

My mother was an angel on the earth. She was a professional musician, a teacher, and a pianist. There was always some little kid sitting at the piano with my mother taking lessons.

I didn't learn to play, but when my mom played, I would stand and listen to her. It was so beautiful, but as a young guy I had a misconception of what a tough guy was, and I didn't want to learn that music.

In my early years I did pretty near everything. I was a bodyguard, a bartender, a horseshoer, a racehorse trainer. I shod horses for twenty years. If my angel wife hadn't been willing to work and share the load, we would have had hell. She always was the reason that we got along.

Did you go to Hollywood as a horseshoer?

Yeah, I was shoeing horses around there, and they made a movie called *Planet of the Apes*. A fellow I was shoeing for had lots of horses he contracted into the movie. They needed some guys to dress up like apes and ride horseback in this movie. He called this casting guy and said, "I've got a guy out here that looks like an ape."

But I never worked in that movie. I was a screen extra and when the call came for me, I was busy.

Then came *The China Syndrome* in 1976. My role was as a nuclear technician in a power plant. I met people like Jack Lemmon and Michael Douglas and a wonderful director named James Bridges. It was a good experience and got me started as an actor.

I've heard you say your favorite role was in The Stone Boy. Why was that?

Well, that was a story about people I like to think I understand. It was about a ranching family in Montana who had a tragic thing happen, and then their personal responses to the experience. There were no heroes in that movie. It was simply a story of tragedy and how people got from the front of it to the back of it and still held themselves together.

Was that the first time you had worked with Robert Duvall?

Oh, no. The first time I worked with Bob Duvall was—well maybe it was the first time. My memory is getting short. We did *The*

Wilford Brimley

Natural and *Tender Mercies*. He's the best actor we got in America, I know that.

> ***My friend, you don't take a back seat to anybody—I think you're one of the best actors in the world. One of my favorite things you did was* The Natural. *Then you and Richard Farnsworth did a television show together that I wish had gone on.***

Yeah, that was *The Boys of Twilight*. But here again, you have to be of a certain mindset and social persuasion to appreciate that kind of thing. We didn't have any incest, any interracial sex or any of that kind of stuff. It was just two old boys trying to do their job. I guess to the hip people that was kind of boring.

> ***I know you have a tremendous love for horses. Do you still breed some mares?***

I'll probably do that until I die. I am pretty fussy about my horses. I like a seven-eighths or fifteen-sixteenths Thoroughbred/Quarterhorse cross. There's air under them. They can get across the ground pretty good without jarring my old kidneys or hips too bad.

I'm not in the cattle business now, but I'm thinking about going back in it. I had a little place on the Snake River in Idaho and got along pretty good for a while. Then for some reason, the federal government took after me, and I ain't in it anymore.

> ***Now, Wilford, we don't have federal lands in Texas. I believe you're the first person I've ever had a chance to talk to who can tell us what it's like to lease federal lands and tell us what all the problems are.***

We have a new breed of bureaucrat today. What we're talking about is less than 2 percent of the population that feeds all of America and most of the world. But people don't understand what it takes.

In the Rocky Mountain West where I come from for some reason the federal government claims ownership to well over seventy-five percent of the land. Historically, those of us in the cow business would get a hold of a little piece of deeded ground—a couple hundred acres—and then we were entitled to run on the government land for a fee.

It was a common misconception that the fees were too cheap. But the fact of the matter is the fees we pay the government for that land is about all we can stand when you stop and consider that in that country a lot of times it takes 225 acres for a cow unit.

The last count was 1,800 special interest groups in Washington, and they're gunning for us and they're winning. I'm not here to say there aren't good people in the Sierra Club and the Audubon Society. But the Indians had a saying, "Don't judge me until you've walked in my moccasins." I think that's pretty wise counsel for anybody.

I'm just sure as anything that it's a cyclical thing, and I'm just sorry I'm caught in that cycle. A century ago, the best estimate I've heard was there were thirty million buffalo on the western plain. They did what the cattle do now. They provide the impetus for cultivation and re-seeding. So they're an asset to the range, rather than a detriment.

I don't guess that you and I can sit here and solve the problems that the livestock operator has with the federal government. But I do think a lot more people need to know the real truth.

In defense of those people, I think they are misinformed. But they don't feel that way. They think they have a solution to a problem that really doesn't exist.

The cowmen in the West have been looking after this country from day one, and it's to their advantage to keep looking after it. It's the way they raise their families, send their kids to college.

I'm sure there are cowmen who violate this wonderful ground, but to say we all devastate the rangeland, we're wanton killers of harmless animals—that's a little too general for me.

(Interviewed in 1996)

SAM WALDSTEIN

I have been lots of places in this old world, but I don't think I have ever seen a more beautiful countryside than the Wichita Mountain Wildlife Refuge outside of Lawton, Oklahoma. It is the perfect setting for the preservation of three uniquely American animal species. The buffalo, the elk, and the longhorn look as though they belong there. This refuge has been a major force in the preservation of the American bison and the perpetuation and preservation of the Texas Longhorn.

Sam Waldstein was very gracious in allowing this interview as well as very hospitable in showing my brother Danny and me around. It was a great day at the refuge.

I was interested in how the refuge got started, so that was the first question I asked.

It's the oldest refuge in the country. In 1901, before Oklahoma was a state, a group of ranchers in Texas and southern Oklahoma and the Native Americans wanted the area preserved and not broken up into small chunks. The Forest Service was the only federal agency available, and they came in and took over the property and made it a national wildlife preserve. Today we primarily have buffalo, Longhorn cattle, elk, deer, some mountain lions, turkey and a few prairie dog towns.

Sam, let's talk about the buffalo.

In 1907 there were very few buffalo left in the United States. The New York Zoological Society wanted to start a new herd. They

Sam Waldstein

shopped around and found a few animals here and there and brought the best ones here to start the first new herd at that time. There were just a few wild ones left in Yellowstone National Park and Canada at that time.

You handle these animals totally different than you would cattle. They are wild, and there is no such thing as a friendly bull buffalo. They have no fear of horses and very little fear of vehicles. The helicopter is the one thing they do not like, and they'll move away from that. That's what we use to round them up.

Their only natural predator was the wolf, so they have a fear of the dog family. If we get some real roughs ones, we use dogs to bunch them up and round them up in a group.

The equipment we use has a lot heavier frame than normal livestock handling equipment. The buffalo have a tendency not to want to stop. If you don't slow them down, they'll hit the metal doors. They tend to challenge the doors. Once they hit a door, they'll hit it again and again. When we bring them into the alleyways and happen to hit them, they'll turn around immediately to defend. They will challenge and fight whatever is there. And they have tremendous jumping ability, so you stay back from the pens.

How long will a cow have calves?

They'll have calves until they're twenty years old, but we usually sell them when they're twelve to fifteen, even though they probably could have calves for a number of years after that.

I have some friends in the buffalo business, and they say the bulls get really cantankerous when they get about eight or nine years old.

We've got kind of an unusual herd because we keep as many bulls as we do cows. Some of the more mature bulls get killed during the season because they fight for dominance. There's a constant period when they fight one another to see which one will be dominant. Usually when they're eight, nine, or ten years old, they tend to go off by themselves and do not join the herd again. They'll just stay off by themselves and never come back in again.

I'm sure that this was the natural order of things because this is one of the few places we keep a natural herd with that many mature bulls. Their prime is five to eight years old and after that they can't compete with the bulls in their prime age. In the natural world, they probably just moved off by themselves and found a pond and had no reason to leave. There were no predators to challenge them, so they just stayed in one area.

Let's talk about Longhorn cattle. As a breed and bloodline, several people had a hand in rescuing the Longhorn. This refuge was one of the main proponents of keeping the breed alive. How did you start the herd and where did it come from?

Well, about 1927 people began to recognize the Longhorn was a unique species and wanted to protect the bloodline. We got some of the people who knew the most about Longhorns at that time and took them to southern Texas and New Mexico to bring the most typical Longhorns back.

Now we have the only Texas Longhorns on any national land. We're real careful to make sure we don't lose any bloodlines. Anytime we sell an animal, we make sure the bloodline is in at least one or two other animals on the refuge. And we store semen, so if we lose a group of animals we can bring them back.

We have a Longhorn sale every third Thursday in September. We sell the oldest and the youngest. The oldest cows are usually fifteen or sixteen years old. We also will donate bulls if we have enough of that bloodline.

This land was part of the Comanche reservation, wasn't it?

Yes, all the southwestern part was one area with Comanches and Wichitas and others living there. In 1901, the land was withdrawn so it never became available for private ownership.

That was the Dawes Act, wasn't it? As I understand it, when the government pulled back the land, they gave every man, woman, and child 160 acres. And then the rest of the land was opened for homestead. Today, we don't have Comanche or Kiowa reservations, so the ranchers came in and bought that from those families, is that correct?

Yes, the land was available for sale. For long periods ranchers like Quanah Parker, the Comanche chief, lived nearby and they had a lot of the Comanche land that they controlled.

A lot of the Texas ranchers came up and paid him. They were good friends. He leased land to them, and they had the right to sell it, so there are no really large pieces of Native American land now.

One of the larger chunks of land the Comanche Nation has now is right beside the refuge. We want them to develop a buffalo herd, and last year we gave them twenty calves. Their attachment to the buffalo is unique.

Once when I was over there working with them on another agreement for herbs and plants from the refuge, I mentioned we could donate buffalo. It was just amazing the interest level. We donated twenty last year and another twenty this year and then they'll establish their own herds.

Sam, I once read a letter in the Panhandle-Plains Museum from Quanah Parker to Charles Goodnight. He was going to Texas and wanted to bring some braves by the ranch to look at buffalo and make some old Indian hearts glad. That's one of the most emotional things I've ever read from any Indian to a white man. They really missed the buffalo.

Now let's talk about the elk. Were they naturally a plains animal?

Yes, they were one of most widespread animals in United States when early settlement came in. Over time, because of the size of the animal, they were hunted out. They don't really know what species was here then. They could have been out of New Mexico or Manitoba.

That's not the species we have here now. We got these from the Rocky Mountain herds. That's the one we established around 1910 or 1911. It's a little different animal from the one that was originally here. Because of their size, they were a valuable food source and were hunted aggressively.

The wildlife refuge is on federal land north of Lawton, Oklahoma, and is open to the public. Is that correct?

Yes, we get a million and a half visitors a year. They can hike wherever they want. There's everything from wide open flat spaces to as rough a rock climbing as you would ever want. There's also a youth campground and a wilderness camp.

(Interviewed in 2001)

DEAN SMITH

Close to forty years ago, I met a young stunt man and actor in Hollywood, California. I remember I especially had a warm feeling toward him because he was a fellow Texan, and at that time, I felt like I was lost in the forest of the movie world. As time went on, Dean and I became better acquainted through our mutual friends, Ben Johnson, Wilford Brimley, Richard Farnsworth, and Robert Totten. We have been close friends for at least thirty of those forty years.

Dean was a great stuntman, is a great actor, and at one time, was one of the fastest men on earth. Not many people know that Dean Smith won a gold medal in the Olympics. His athletic ability, even today, takes good care of him. He understands horses about as good as anybody I know and does a wonderful job of training horses to do things that lots of folks don't even consider possible for a horse to do.

Dean has moved back to Texas. He and his wife Debbie and their son, Finnis, live out west of Fort Worth in a part of the country where Dean grew up. I will always consider Dean Smith one of my closest and dearest friends.

I know about where you grew up but I'd like for you to tell folks.

I was born in Breckenridge, Texas, in 1932. My grandparents came from Weatherford in about 1870 to the Clear Fork of the Brazos. We've got land there, and that's where I learned to rope and ride. Like most boys who grew up in the Depression, our biggest pleasure was going to the movies on a Saturday and seeing Roy and Gene and Tex Ritter and all those guys.

I remember just a half a mile from here I used to raise chickens. I would take the eggs to the A&P store and sell them and use that money to go to the movies. That kind of instilled a lot of things in me.

When I was a boy I always wanted to be a cowboy. I rode my first bucking horse at the Texas Cowboy Reunion in Stamford, Texas. I was left-handed and not too good of a roper, but I rode a bareback horse real well.

When I was about sixteen, my grandmother decided we were going to move to Graham. We moved next door to a coach, and he got me out for football and found out I could run. The first year I ran track I was a state high school champion and made *Look* magazine all-American track team.

After my junior year in high school, I started getting offers from just about everybody in the whole country, like Notre Dame, USC, and all the Southwest Conference schools. But I had gone to a track meet at Laredo and met Clyde Littlefield. I knew I needed a little more coaching, and he could give it to me, so I chose the University of Texas.

I went there on a full track scholarship. He taught me how to run, and I won eight Southwest Conference individual titles. I also played football my freshman, sophomore and junior years. They didn't really want me to play football because they thought I would get hurt. That didn't bother me any, but I didn't play my senior year.

Instead, I took care of Bevo, the Longhorn steer mascot. I remember taking Willie Morris, who was a famous author and writer from Mississippi, with me to Notre Dame to a football game.

I'll never forget, when I led Bevo into the stadium at South Bend, those people just went crazy. That was better than running track and playing football.

***I have never interviewed anyone who owns an Olympic
gold medal until now. I have to have you tell us about it.***

Well, the Lord blessed me with this natural ability. I went to the Sugar Bowl track meet in 1952 and beat a boy from Georgia Tech. I ran the 100 meters in 10.3 seconds. I just kept working and working

Dean Smith

and went to California and won nationals at Long Beach and made the Olympic team.

It was during the Cold War and we were competing against the Russians. We really wanted to win. We marched into that stadium and we were proud of who we were. We were Americans. I ran the 100 meter dash, and there were six of us in the finish. We all had a 10.4, and they gave me fourth.

Three days later we beat those Russians in a relay, and I got a gold medal. I was twenty years old. There's not a day that goes by that somebody doesn't say something about that Olympic medal. To this very day, I'm just really proud of that medal. Any time you talk about the Olympics, it's a prestigious thing.

That medal has done so much for me. In those days you couldn't take money, but it opened a lot of doors. But it wasn't the money, it was the people I associated with and met who made things nice for me.

Dean, let's touch on a few things that first happened to you when you went to Hollywood.

The first thing that happened to me was I spent twenty-one months in the Army. While I was out there I went to Hollywood and met Bud McFadin, who was an All-America at Texas. He talked me into signing with the Los Angeles Rams.

I got there, and he was ill and didn't show up. Later they wanted to send me to Pittsburgh, but I didn't want to go. It was too cold back East, and I wanted to be near Hollywood.

I finally decided to leave and got in my car and drove back to Breckenridge. About a week later, I picked up the *Dallas Morning News*, and there was a picture of James Garner. He had done the pilot on *Maverick*, and I told my mother I was going to go there and ask him if he could get me in the movies. I went down there, and within ten days I was back in Hollywood. That's how I got my start.

After Jim Garner got me in pictures, I went on my way and started working. I had to get my foot in the door. I had met Dale Robertson, who was doing *Tales of Wells Fargo*. I said I knew he probably had a double, but if he ever had a need to change, I'd like a chance to double him. He said okay.

He got blood poisoning in his foot, and within two weeks I was working for him. And forty-four years later we're still the best of friends. He's always been there when I needed him. He's just kinfolk

Dean Smith and Red

to me. There's not anything that we haven't done. He is the nicest gentleman and has a lot of class.

After I started working for him, they were going to make a movie in 1959 called *The Alamo*. Being from Texas, I wanted to be in it. John Wayne was producing it and directing it, and I got a chance to work on it.

They had a shot where Tennesseans had to go and steal Longhorn cattle. I ran and jumped over a horse like a hurdler over a fence. It turned out a great, great shot and gave me a reputation.

This man was standing there, and he said his name was John Ford. He said he had never seen anybody doing anything like that before and from then on I could work on all his pictures—and I did. I worked on *Two Rode Together, Cheyenne Autumn, How the West Was Won*. I doubled Ben Johnson on *Cheyenne Autumn* when he dropped a trailer on his foot and broke it.

How was John Ford to work for?
We read all kinds of different accounts.

I think he knew I was a naïve country boy from Texas. He'd put the pressure on me, but it made me do better work. He didn't put the needle on you or kid you unless he cared a lot about you. I was the last young man to be in the John Ford stock company.

What impressed me most was that you guys were
a great big family.

Red, you and I come from an era when we cared about people. The thing is, it was the same way with that stock company. We loved and respected each other, and we knew there was a loyalty there.

Now, a lot of times I work on something and other than getting the money, it's not the same. The caring and loyalty we had in those days meant something.

When you were working on these pictures, there was a man out
there I knew named Glenn Randall. Tell us about him.

He let me in on a little of his secrets, but he didn't tell me all of them. I learned a lot from him. He trained Trigger and all those horses on *Ben Hur*. In 1977 I wanted to play Tom Mix myself. I had the ability, but I never was able to raise the money.

I bought a gelding named Sunday and took him to Glenn and left him there for about a year. He later was voted the cleverest horse at Universal pictures.

Then Dale gave me a horse called Hollywood. I spent six months with Glenn, and he taught me a lot of things about horses. I have nothing but great respect for him. There is never going to be another guy like Glenn Randall.

Where do you think he learned it?

I think he probably learned a lot of what he knew from the circus, and it probably came from Europe. He was a really smart guy. You can't do what he did without having a lot of intelligence.

I've heard you tell a lot of stories about Hollywood.
Lay some on us.

People came in there from all walks of life, but the people who impressed me most were the cowboys and all the people who worked in Westerns. A lot of people wanted me to ride motorcycles and do all kinds of things, but I just wanted to do Westerns.

The hardest thing I did wasn't the stunts, but getting the job. That's the hardest thing I ever did. As long as we were working on pictures, things were great. But unless we were working, it wasn't the kind of place where I wanted to be. I got there in 1957 when things were really good. But by the time I left in 1992, they had quit making the Western pictures. I think a lot of it was because guys like John Wayne and Gary Cooper and Jimmy Stewart, all those great guys, loved their work.

I found out that making Westerns is like a good cake or pie. If you have a good recipe, don't change it. You can't change a good Western. You need good horses, good stunt people, and Western people who know what they're doing.

But also, those stories had good story lines and good ethics and good morals. Most of the really good pictures came from actual events. One of the great movies of all times was *The Alamo*. John Wayne produced and directed it. It was a large production and one of my favorites. It was my first big picture, and you can imagine how excited I was coming back to Texas.

In the movie, I doubled Frankie Avalon and I had fifteen costumes. I did fancy jumps and double horse falls with Bill Williams, who was doubling Richard Widmark. It was a terrific movie to work on. I had fifteen lines in a movie that was more than three hours. In one scene, Laurence Harvey looked up at me and asked if the cannon was ready. I said "The gun is ready, sir. All primed and ready, sir."

I'll never forget one day we were just about to break at twelve o'clock and this great big plane landed. It was carrying Darrell Royal, Emory Bellard, all the coaches from UT. They wanted to see Dean Smith. I thought Duke Wayne was going to fire me over that.

*You know, Dean, the thing that's kept the image of the West alive
is the music and the pictures on television and motion pictures.
Hollywood has prostituted a wonderful way of life and shown
things about the cowboy that didn't exist. I really wish we could
make movies again that show there is a definite difference
between right and wrong, there's no gray areas.*

Red, you know my heroes have always been cowboys. I've always
been a cowboy, and I wish every little kid in this country could have
had the bringing up that you and I had because I do believe Westerns
taught us fair play and taught us right from wrong.

I want to know about you doubling
Maureen O'Hara in McClintock.

Boy, that was a good one. In 1961, I had already done *Comancheros*
and had doubled one girl. First, I was told I had to go to Max Factor
and got a big red wig. Then I went to wardrobe and got white tights
and padding. All day long, I was falling off a ladder into a water trough
or running up and down the streets with John Wayne chasing me.

And the stuntmen, boy they kidded me like you wouldn't believe.
I had to double Maureen and Strother Martin in a big mud fight, and
it was a cold day. They had drilling mud out there, and we got it in
our nose and our ears, and boy we had a time.

Did Maureen O'Hara slide down that mud?

She damn sure did. She was a good old girl. When they did a com-
memorative coin on John Wayne, I was invited to Washington, and I
went with her and some others. That was one of the highlights of my life.

We've talked about falling horses, and I want to really get
into that. Tell us how they made those horses fall.

Well, back around 1936 or '37 they did a picture called *The
Charge of the Light Brigade.* They did pitfalls. Horses would run in
them and they would turn them upside down and they would
injure a lot of horses.

They were just doing things through brute strength. Even when
they did *Jesse James* with Tyrone Powers and Henry Fonda, they

shoved a lot of horses off cliffs. They would blindfold them and push them down a chute and they would fall seventy to eighty feet.

Finally, people started getting civilized and thought that was inhumane, so about that time Yakima Canutt and all those guys knew they were going to have to start being better to horses.

I learned how to train horses and put down sand so they wouldn't be hurt. We learned we could tie up a front leg and wrap a bit with rubber so it wouldn't hurt the horse's mouth. They were trained to go down very easy. Then we trained them at a walk and then a trot, then a gallop and then a run. It's just a process. They got it so perfected, it was terrific.

Did you do any high falls?

Yes, but I didn't take to it too much when I first started. About the highest I had ever been was on the back of a horse, and that was pretty high when he started bucking. You get up about twenty feet, and we had little old cardboard boxes and mattresses—it was easy to miss one of those. But now, as I reached the end of my career, they started coming up with those big old pads and airbags.

I was very fortunate when I started working with Dale Robertson and John Ford and John Wayne and all those guys because they had great talent. I got on-the-job training from them.

All of them, not only the stuntmen, but the horse people, they knew horses. They were used to doing all those great chases with stagecoaches and bank robberies. That was just a way of life. Those people were descendants, just like you and I, of the pioneers. They had a flavor for all that stuff.

What are you doing with your horses today?

I do things with kids at schools. I go and take my trick horse and do a few things every once in a while. I do celebrity cuttings and ropings—things like that. And a few golf tournaments. My golf's not very good, but I sure do get to associate with a lot of good ol' boys.

I fell in love with Longhorn cattle, and I've had them for about seventeen or eighteen years. I have everybody in the world trying to tell me that I shouldn't have Longhorns. But, you know we've been in a drought here for three or four years. I've still got my cows, and everybody else has sold theirs three or four times.

They're very durable, but if I was in a business to make a living with cows and horses, I'd starve to death.

(Interviewed in 2000)

DALE ROBERTSON

I have known Dale Robertson almost as long as I have known Dean Smith, Ben Johnson, Richard Farnsworth, and Wilford Brimley. We have been going to the same golf and roping functions for a long, long time. I think Dale Robertson is the epitome of a Western actor. He not only has a strong, handsome face and physique, but he carries himself with an air of confidence that everyone likes to think was common to the Western man. Dale will long be remembered for his exploits and his roles in the motion picture and television industry. But I have a feeling that he would rather be remembered as the world class horseman that he is. He loves horses more than just about anybody I know. And in his lifetime, has bred some of the most outstanding animals the horse world has ever seen. Dale is a very special friend of mine, and I treasure that relationship. When I interviewed him, I started like I always do by asking him about his background.

I was born about twenty miles east of Oklahoma City in Harrah, most famous because you spell it the same way backward and forward. We were raised on a farm, which I still think is the greatest way to raise children. We loved animals and learned to work. I'd pick cotton or chop cotton, but Dad made me quit because I cut down more cotton plants than I did weeds.

How did you get interested in horses?
I started at McCloud. They had match raises and rode what they called catch weight—that's anything that's alive and breathing. I was

Dale Robertson

only five years old. We'd go just as hard as we could and never could stop those horses.

Horses became my life. Without knowing it, when I was eight years old, I did the right thing. I set a goal for myself. I said I was going to breed the greatest horse the world had ever known, and from that day on I never woke up and said, "I wonder what I'll do today." I had every day planned out and filled, all with the horses.

I started this farm with five mares. Each of them was a world champion or the dam of a world champion in something. I remember I bought a horse I called Hi Dale. I saw her out in the middle of a pasture in Carlsbad, New Mexico, and stopped and got out and walked over there.

The owner came out to see what I was doing and recognized me. I told him he had a good mare, and he said I had a good eye because she had just set the world record at 400 yards. I asked him if he wanted to sell her, and he said he guessed he would if the price were right. When I asked him what the right price was, he said, 'How about $9,000?' So I bought her, and she was in foal with a horse called Three Bars.

Her colt was called Spanish Fort and had to be examined by two inspectors from the American Quarterhorse Association. The first one that came out said, "Dale, this is the only perfect horse I've ever seen." Then another one came and looked him over and said he couldn't find any faults. He became the three-year-old champion.

I don't know if you know the history of the All-American Futurity, but it started with me talking to a friend in a restaurant who had a horse, Steamship, bred to Be Sure Now. I told him I believed I had him beat, and he suggested we match up. We sat there and wrote it out on a napkin, and then another man who was sitting there wanted in on it. So we all decided to put up $10,000 each, winner take all. And, boy, the word spread so fast you couldn't believe it.

We finally shut it off at ten. Next thing, the track heard about it and wanted to hold it at Ruidoso, New Mexico, and we thought that's where it should be. So we all sat around trying to come up with a name. I said, "We're all Americans and we all love this country, so why don't we call it the 'All-American Futurity,'" and that's where it was born.

Those of us, and there were millions, who saw you in the rodeo arena doing your show fell in love with your horse, Jubilee. How old was he when you retired him?

He was twenty-two, but his story didn't end there. The old man who took care of him for me took him home and looked after him. He called and said his daughter wanted to make a hunter out of him. She took him and made a champion hunter out of him.

He did any job you asked him to do. He had his little quirks like when I'd first come to work he wanted to run. So I'd take him out in the hills and we'd run. If I was late to work and didn't have time, he was grouchy and crabby all day long.

***I'd love to spend all of our time talking about horses,
but I want you to tell us how you got to Hollywood
and got into the acting business.***

Well, before World War II there was a hell of a Depression on, and
we did anything we had to do in order to make a living. I was fighting in the amateurs. One night a fellow asked my brother if he was
my manager, and my brother said he was. This fellow said he would
like to manage me, and my brother agreed.

So we started fighting, and he started teaching me to be a count-
er-fighter. He said I could whip anybody I could get to come over to
me. That was our secret—how to get them to come after us and
chase us. Then when they started hollering, *pretty boy*, he said, "Do
you want to be a world's champion or do you want to make money?
The thing you've got to do is use them and not let them use you. They
want to call you *pretty boy*, go along with it and act like you're afraid
to get hit in the face."

The first time they booed me, I didn't like it. But before long, I was
getting a charge out of boos, because I knew I was doing it right.

One night, a guy said he wanted to talk to me. He was from
Columbia Pictures and wanted to take me to dinner.

He said they were going to make a picture called *Golden Boy*,
which he said I was perfect for. But I was only seventeen years old
and trying to build a farm and train horses and go to school. I said I
didn't think my mother would let me, so I didn't go. I didn't regret it
and never thought anymore about it.

During the war, I was stationed at St. Luis Obispo, and I called
Mom and asked what she wanted for Christmas. She wanted a nice
picture made, so I went to Hollywood to get a picture made. There
were fourteen of us there, and we all went.

A lady by the name of Harriet Parsons was there, and we told her
we all wanted portraits to send home to our families for Christmas.
We told her we probably weren't going to be there, so she was going
to have to take down our names and addresses and pick out the best
portrait and send it.

So we left, and I was in North Africa. I started getting all these letters from Hollywood wanting me to make pictures. I told my com-

manding officer, "They want me to make pictures out there in Hollywood, and I think I'd like to go." He said, "Yeah, well, Uncle Sam really needs you severely over here in North Africa."

So that was that. I didn't get to go to Hollywood and make my big career. Finally, the war was over, and we went home. I was wounded and couldn't fight anymore. I just went out and started looking for work and couldn't find anything.

I was sitting down one night going through all the letters I had gotten while I was in the war, and I ran across one of those letters from Hollywood. I thought that would be as good a job as any if a fellow could get started at it. So I left to try to get enough money to get my farm back and get some horses. I got a lot of opportunities, but I couldn't find the right part. But I knew I had the law of averages working for me.

I was right. The part of Jesse James came up in the *Fighting Man of the Plains* and that got me started. I went down to the screening in Long Beach. When I made my appearance, a rumble went through the crowd, and when I made my second appearance another rumble went through the crowd. Now I had offers from everybody in town.

I was signed to a picture with Fox, but then Darryl Zanuck and I had a falling out over a script called *The Girl in the Red Velvet Swing*.

He said there was a new actress in England named Angela Lansbury who was very, very popular who was going to be in it. But she dropped out, and after I read the script I could see why. It was about husbands running around on their wives. I told them I wouldn't do the picture, either, and then they came to me with another script that was the same thing.

I told them I didn't believe in married men running around on their wives, and I wasn't going to be a part of a campaign to tell everyone it's all right.

Tell us how Wells Fargo came about.

When they first sent me the *Wells Fargo* script, I said I couldn't do it. I already had commitments and didn't like the script. They rewrote it, and it wasn't any better. Then they sent it back a third time, and I saw where we could make a few changes. I didn't think we would ever sell that pilot even with a few changes, but the first ones we showed it to bought it. Seven years later I was trying to get back to doing features.

Then I did another series called *The Iron Horse* that lasted 47 episodes.

Now I know one of the really important things to you were the horses that you used in those pictures. Tell us about some of the horse trainers and some of the special talents they had.

Ralph McCutcheon was one of the best of all of them. Ralph taught them out of kindness and gentleness. Glenn Randall used whips. He was a great trainer, but I liked the way Ralph trained. I think his horses performed better, too.

Who were some of the actors and actresses you remember?

My favorite big star was Betty Grable. I was at Fox the same time she was. She loved animals and was so good and kind to everybody. All the crew, everybody loved her.

Gary Cooper was my all-time favorite male star. He was a good friend. Clark Gable and Bob Taylor were, too.

Like millions of other Americans, I wanted to know what kind of guy was Gary Cooper. He was everybody's hero.

He was the best you'd ever want to know. He was pretty smart, too. He had a little gimmick going. He had his name on his checks with a line, "If not cashed within 30 days, this check becomes null and void." Every year, they'd move $80,000 to $100,000 over to a separate account. He wrote checks for everything. If he bought $3 worth of gas, he'd write a check for it.

People weren't going to get rid of them. They wanted to keep them. The government wanted to tax him for that money that was in the bank. He said, "No, that's not my money. If they ever send them through, I've got to make them good."

He had to pay tax on the interest, but they never did get the tax on the principle. It was a great gimmick.

I tried it, and, hell, they cashed mine before they got out the door.

Victor Mature was at Fox when I was there, too. He was a nice fellow, but we never were very close. Ty Powers and I were close, and Leslie Howard.

I know that Oklahoma holds a very special place in your heart. Tell us about your life back home in Oklahoma.

When I came back I had ideas for stories but no time to write them. I learned to type on a computer and now write screenplays. I don't have a good enough vocabulary to write books, but maybe someday I can get someone to transpose those over into a book.

I'm not doing anything with horses now. They were part of my life for over sixty years. If I go back I'll probably go into the pleasure horse business so I can work with kids—I don't need to be racing at this age.

(Interviewed in 2000)

BARRY CORBIN

I have known Barry Corbin for approximately twenty years. He is a very special friend and I consider him to be one of the great actors of our time. Barry loves West Texas and all its history, its stories, and its people. His portrayal of Charles Goodnight is pretty spooky because he looks and acts just like Charlie. Barry loves horses and is quite an accomplished cutting horse rider. He has a large number of belt buckles that attest to his prowess on the back of a horse. Since I always like to find out where a person came from, I started off the interview by letting Barry tell us about his background. Here's what he said:

I was raised out by Lamesa. Somebody accused me of imitating Ben Johnson, the way we talked, and Ben said, "No, we just ate the same kind of dust when we were kids."

I used to go every Saturday afternoon to watch Bill Elliott or one of those guys catch the bad guys and that's where I got the idea that's what I wanted to do when I grew up.

My granddad had been a cowboy and rancher, and he moved to West Texas to raise cotton. But he always had a few calves around and an old horse or two. I grew up riding bad horses, and I never rode a good horse until I was fifty."

What did you do in your younger years that made you the great actor you are and made you love the Western way of life?
I wanted to do Western movies when I grew up, but I got side-tracked in kind of a funny way. When I was in high school and college

Barry Corbin

I started doing Shakespeare. When I moved to New York, I did a lot of English plays, Shakespeare, and that kind of thing.

I was stubborn. I'm glad now I was because this is my living now. When you get a little older, you start trying to simplify your life and get back to what your roots are. Mine are in Texas.

Barry Corbin, right, with Red, Tom Selleck, cowboy singer Don Edwards

I went to college at Texas Tech, except for one summer I went to the University of Colorado where they have a Shakespeare festival. You have to be a student to be in it, and they give you a room and a meal ticket, plus $15 to $20 a week spending money. I didn't like the fellow I was living with, so I went to a ranch outside Boulder and offered to work there in return for a place to live. So I was probably the only fellow stringing fences in the morning and playing in *As You Like It* at night."

Tell us when you really got into the Western part of the movies.

I moved to California, and couldn't get anybody to look at me. I paid my rent by writing radio plays for National Public Radio. I would write parts in it for me. They paid me $200 for the script, and then they paid the actors $100. So I would write parts that nobody else could play but me.

I was doing a play that I wrote called *Suckerrod Smith and the Cisco Kid*, based on a real person out in Lamesa. My agent called me up and told me to go to Paramount where they were casting *Urban Cowboy*. There was a big part for John Travolta's uncle. I figured they would hire Ben Johnson or somebody like that, but they liked me and called my agent back. The way I knew I had the part was that they gave me a new pair of Tony Lama boots to break in. I knew they wouldn't give me those boots if I didn't have the part.

It didn't every really sink in on me that I had the part until we got down to Houston. It was a very exciting time for me—it was almost like my life had been pointed toward that moment. In a way it was kind of a letdown. In a movie you sit around a lot and then do three or four lines and then sit around. The process really is the same for working on the stage or working on film or television. There's just a different time value.

Do you remember any unusual things that happened on that set?

Most of the people were locals who hung around in Gilley's. They weren't used to being treated like cattle, shoved around into holding areas. I was walking past this guy named Norman, who was an extra in the show, and he didn't like it.

I told him not to hit the man he was mad at because he would get sued. The guy he was talking about turned out to be a hotshot producer who later hired me. He asked me if I remembered him and I said, "I sure do remember you, and if it hadn't been for me you wouldn't be here today."

Let's get into something that is near and dear to your heart and mine and the hearts of Western fans all over the world. I think we can safely say that from the day Lonesome Dove was on the air, it was the benchmark for Westerns from that time. Would you agree?

I agree completely. My father, who is kind of an amateur Western historian, was visiting me in California when it premiered. They showed two parts, which was three and a half hours, then they took a dinner break for an hour and a half and came back and showed the second half, which was another three and a half hours. I figured my dad would be good for maybe half of the first bunch.

But in those first three and a half hours, he never even got up to go have a smoke. When it came time to eat, I asked him if he wanted to leave. He, said, "Hell, no, I want to see the rest of it." He sat through the whole thing, and I knew we had a hit then.

I read the book when it first came out, and I thought it was going to be a mini-series. It was my understanding that Larry McMurtry wrote it as a screenplay for John Wayne, Jimmy Stewart, and Henry Fonda. Then he wrote the novel. I read it and called my agent up and told him to keep an eye out for it.

The first day of shooting was the scene where we meet the young girl out in the woods. I didn't know who was playing Captain Call. I walked into the makeup room and there was a big guy lying there with something over his face. In a minute I heard this big voice, "Welcome home, Barry." I turned around, and it was Tommy Lee Jones.

I was doing a movie called *Who's Harry Crumb?*, where I was playing one of the richest guys in the world. That was a nice juxtaposition, since I was playing one of the poorest in *Lonesome Dove*.

Was Conagher *next?*

Well, *Conagher* was a little later, but that was kind of an interesting thing. I got to the location in Colorado and the stunt coordinator asked me if I could drive a six-up. I said "No," and he said, "You do now."

So I spent three days trying to drive six horses. Fortunately, it was a good team, but your hands have to be so strong to drive them. They can nearly jerk you out of the box when they take off.

First thing, I was loping them on a rise, and I had to turn them to the left and start on a mark and talk. Nobody told me the hay wagon was to the right, and I was supposed to turn to the left.

The lead team started veering to the right, and I started grabbing slack. They started veering back slowly to the left. As they came back around, I was looking over their ears and saw the man on B camera looking over the camera, poised to run.

***Don't you think that* Lonesome Dove *and* Dances With Wolves**
were wonderful portrayals of the American Western lifestyle?
And don't you think that a lot of Westerns have been done
poorly because most of the movie industry does not understand
or identify with Westerns?

That's right, Red. The public loves them, but the people who make the decisions don't identify with them, don't care for them, and never have. I've got a theory on that—I think they're afraid of the wranglers.

Let's talk about television. When we were growing up we watched
shows like* Leave it to Beaver, Father Knows Best *and all the
Westerns that were on television at that time. There was a life les-
son in every single show. As time went on, we lost a lot of that and
just got around to trying to shock folks with language.
In* Northern Exposure, *it was not only the lives of the people,
but it was a very wholesome show. The things you guys had
to say were wholesome things.

Yes, I don't know what the other people on the show felt, but I feel that when you do a series, there's a leap of faith between you and the writers and producers. I signed to do a character. In anything else, it's going to be essentially what you see. You have no idea what's going to happen down the road. You have to fight for the integrity of your character. There's an example of that in *Vera Cruz* with Burt Lancaster and Gary Cooper.

In the original script, Gary Cooper went into a climactic gunfight and got the girl. They got down to Mexico and changed the script so that Cooper and Lancaster drew at the same time and killed each other.

Cooper tore that page out of the script, wrote something on it, ordered a bottle of tequila and walked out of the dining room. Scrawled across that paper was 'Coop don't die.'

It was very astute because people would not accept him dying. He had an image he had to maintain. People expect certain things of certain people. Once you have a reputation you'd better be real careful about preserving it.

That's one of the reasons *Northern Exposure* maintained its integrity up until the last season.

I've seen you do something that goes back to your days on the stage. You're absolutely brilliant in your portrayal of Col. Charles Goodnight in the play, The Last Night of Goodnight's Life. Do you have a chance to do that very often?

No, I don't do it as often as I would like to. It's something I really love doing. Goodnight was a tough, hard, profane old man. But he had so much grit and intelligence and drive. The things that he went through, I don't know a man now who could live through it.

He was such a strong presence. We toyed with the idea of cleaning him up a little bit for the play. But we decided not to because it wouldn't be true to him. It was part of his character.

We don't know what his voice sounded like, but I suspect that it's pretty close to what I play. He was from southern Illinois, and they sound pretty much like we do. When he was a young man, people were given to much more flowery phraseology than we are today.

I watched some silent film of him and got some of his gestures. He was never at rest in his life, I think. He was constantly working from the time he would get up in the morning until he couldn't see at night.

When he was an old man he talked about his work not being done. He was a botanist and was interested in all kinds of wildlife. He was so dedicated to life that I think that's why he lived so long. And to him life was work and work was life.

Think of all the things he did. He was a Texas Ranger and Army scout. He was an innovator. Everything about him was inventive.

The last poem in Andy Wilkinson's book is called "Saddlin' Up Time." He said, "I'm damned if I'll go before it's saddlin' up time." Goodnight died just before saddlin' up time on Dec. 12, 1929.

What are some things you would like to do you haven't gotten to do yet?

I've been real lucky. I don't have any immediate specific goals, but I do just want to keep working. I enjoy the process. I've been reading a book, *A Man in Full*, by Tom Wolfe. I'd like to play the central character in that.

A project I've been trying to get going for years is *The Time it Never Rained*, Elmer Kelton's book. I've talked to Elmer about it, but I can't get anybody to do it. Maybe before I get too old I'll be able to do that. There's been scripts written and ideas of doing it. I sure would love to do it if we can ever get anybody to finance it. It's one of those stories that if done right would be like *Lonesome Dove*. It would be on the shelves of every ranch house in the country.

If somebody offered you another series today, would you do it?

Yes, if they did the right one I would. I'm not anxious to do a series, but if the right one came along I would. The problem is, you've got to relocate while they're doing it, and you don't get home very often.

We had an eight-day shooting schedule on *Northern Exposure*, which means we would work Monday through Friday and then the next week we'd work Monday, Tuesday and Wednesday on that same episode. Then on Thursday, we'd start a new episode. We'd shoot from July until April. Then I'd have two months to kind of regroup.

(Interviewed in 1997)

BUSTER WELCH

Like jillions of other folks that know him, I admire Buster Welch more than words can express. He is considered by most people in the know, to be the dean of cutting horse trainers. I know Buster as a trainer, but I know him better as a friend, a cowboy, and a cowman. One of the reasons Buster is such a great cutting horse trainer is because he has the ability to know what cattle are going to do in almost any given situation. He knows horses like the back of his hand. He understands people as well as anybody I have ever known, and we have had a number of memorable nights around the campfire relating stories about the history and the people of our beloved West Texas. I consider Buster a very dear friend and am honored to be included in his circle of acquaintances. I know that he has a colorful background as a cowboy and cowman so I asked him to just begin his story when he was a young man. This is what he said:

I was born in Sterling City, and I grew up and went to school in Midland. I started day working while I was going to school and left home because I didn't see any need for an education.

I saddled a horse one night and rode forty-five miles against a real cold south wind to the Proctors' ranch. That old horse bucked with me and pulled all the buttons off my coat. I rode all night against that wind, but boy I was happy—I was going to be a cowboy.

Things hadn't changed much then. The fences were still there that had been put there in the 1890s. The pastures were big. I know when I went to work for the Xs, the first ten days I was there I didn't see a fence.

Buster and Sheila Welch

They just made drives in those big pastures. The Proctors had some big old country and leased a lot of little ranches and put them together. There was still a lot of cowboying then. Those men really had a lot of skill and grace handling cattle. I look back and marvel at what they could do with cows.

Most of the fences were three-wire fences and a lot of them were just on old mesquite posts that were a long way apart. They had gates, but you never drove a lot of cattle through them. You wouldn't go through a gate with a herd of cows and calves—it would take too long and you would lose some. You would just kick the fence down and drive them through. Then someone would go back and fix the fence.

The pastures were big, and the herds of cattle you threw together were more mixed and wild. All the cattle were fantastically alert back then. You'd throw a roundup together, and there was lots of cutting to do. You needed good horses and good men.

I broke lots of horses, and that was my ticket to get hired on. Young men like myself did the work that men didn't want to do. We jingled horses, which means we gathered horses before daylight.

Sometimes you'd have a bell on a horse, and I learned how to listen for him. You could hear those noises a long way. You'd get down in the low places and that way you could skylight out and see them against the sky. And the noise would drift down in there. You wouldn't ride to the high points then like you would in daylight—you'd ride to the low points.

You could see them and you could hear better. If you knew the pasture, you knew how to stay in the low places and cover that pasture good.

And another thing we did was get wood. The old guys would dig at us for the wood we brought back. They'd say, "What crow did you whip and get her nest?" if you didn't cut that wood big enough.

As a young buck, were you ever a hoodlum or a cook's helper?

No. I'd just get in trouble with the cook. And I would sure hustle and wash his dishes and drag him up wood and try to get back in good graces with him. One time they sent us to take a remuda, and we had told the cook about roping a mule deer. He said there was no way to do that.

We decided we'd catch one and put it in the camp with him. We started back and a great big old buck jumped up between us. We didn't say anything. We roped him immediately, but we had a lot more problems than we thought about.

Buster Welch, left, with Red, Matlock Rose, and Lindy Burch

We finally just bobbed his ears off and tied them together and we were going to throw them on the meat table. The cook saw the ears and grabbed a butcher knife and ran us out of there.

I heard a story about some fruit cocktail.

I hate to tell that story on myself, but I will. We had been up at the Four Sixes all summer, and it was hot and dry. Some of us had gone into town and got a gallon of fruit cocktail and some gingerbread mix. We were sitting out there in the brush, laying down eating with big spoons out of that gallon of cocktail mix, and boy it did taste good.

Someone said there was a tarantula crawling up behind me, and I just turned around and hit it with my reins, and they popped when I did. My mare was standing there asleep and it scared her and she went to bucking through those cattle and started the worst stampede.

There I stood about two inches tall and trying to hide in the grass. I finally got a horse and went after that mare and trailed her three days before I found her.

There was probably two or three hundred cows that got loose, and I wasn't very popular with anybody except the kids.

Let's talk a little bit about the horses. Most people refer to you as the dean of cutting horse trainers, and you really invented a lot of what's done today. You've been a major influence in the cutting horse world. Go back for our listeners and explain how the cutting horse was used in the early days and how it's grown into a major sport.

Boley Brown came out of Illinois when he was about eight years old and was raised by an uncle when his father died. He became a big rancher and loved good horses. Back then the main people who were successful were the ones who could handle cattle, horses, and men because that's all they needed.

They didn't have fences or buildings. All they had was horses, cattle, men, and grass. When they would round-up in that open range, they might go out twenty miles and make a dry camp and get up the next morning and drive those cattle in.

They could have seven or eight thousand cattle, and they'd be mixed. They were limited on the time they could hold those cattle together and sort them. You had to sort them and turn loose the ones you wanted to stay on the ranch.

Boley Brown always said a cowman was just as good as the horses he rode. There couldn't be any stirring of those cattle. They wanted a horse that would move through a set of cattle like a fox in a henhouse. It took a lot of grace to work those big, wild herds of cattle and not get them stirred up.

Boley got up to where he had two hundred horses. They said he would give a cowboy up to $100 for a good cow horse, and you could buy any horse for $50 then.

The whole idea of a cutting horse is to move one individual out of the herd and keep that individual from returning to the herd. A good cutting horse will watch a cow over ten or fifteen other cows by moving her and counter-moving her, always moving to the edge, without causing any disturbance.

What kind of horses were those?

I'm sure they had good bloodlines. The Thoroughbred horses then seemed to have come in on those little Spanish horses, and they were all cow horses. They'd cross those with government remount studs. We got lots of good cow horses out of those.

When we're talking about a horse that's got a lot of cow, we're talking about a horse that has a natural inclination to want to work cattle almost any way you need him to work. But when we're talking about a real cow horse, we're talking about a horse that has a natural inclination to want to be a cutting horse.

It's just bred in him. I've seen some early art from 400 or 500 B.C. that would show horses with their ears back going up to an ox and the guy getting off of it. That horse had cow.

The Indians rode a buffalo horse they got from the Spaniards. They had to put twenty-five arrows in a buffalo to bring him down, and they had to do it with two hands. So that horse had to be full of cow.

A top buffalo horse would bring a hundred ordinary horses. There was one famous sub-chief who carried an extra teepee for his buffalo horse. And his wives cut grass and brought it to him to feed him.

The first recorded cutting contest with prize money was at Haskell, Texas, in 1898, and the contests got pretty popular until the Depression hit the ranching business in about 1925. Then they just quit. They started back up in 1933 at Stamford.

Then they went to fencing the ranches up, and the cutting horse wasn't near as important. Those guys got to sending their kids off to school and educating them instead of teaching them how to work cattle. So cutting liked to have died off from '25 to '33.

It was pretty slow getting off again. They formed the National Cutting Horse Association in '46. Fern Sawyer was quite a cowgirl, and she did a whole lot to get people interested again.

Today there is something like $20 million a year in prize money nationwide.

How many major events have you won in your career?

Oh, I couldn't start to tell you that, but I can tell you some of the highlights. I've won five world championships, five futurities, three derbies, and probably all the major shows they used to have. I know I won Fort Worth three times.

You'd get on a hot streak and you might win ten or fifteen shows in a row back then. They've got some kind of a grading deal, and I think I might have won the most.

Do you remember how much you won at the first futurity?

Yes, that first one I won $3,700. The highest ever won was $225,000, but they can't win that now. They split it up, and now the highest is about $125,000. My son, Greg, has been the high money winner for three years. One year he won $600,000. It beats cowboying.

Let's talk about your ranching operation, the Double Mountain River Ranch. What kind of cattle do you raise?

I run a half-Angus and half-Limousin operation. That's a thrifty kind of a cow. She has a little more vigor and doesn't get near as big as a Limousin would have. You'll get a feeder that has a high yield and also marbles and has a good taste. I'm hitting for a special niche and I'm able to sell my cattle a little higher.

You've got lots of interesting stories, especially some of those escapades with Buddy Clark.

We were working on a ranch between Sterling City and Carlsbad on the Concho River. Buddy knew that country, and I went with him and got a job branding. One evening it started raining, and we were about two-thirds through. We had to turn the cattle loose and went to an old vacant house to wait out the rain.

The boss turned everybody loose but me and Buddy. He said he'd give us a couple of extra days if we'd take the remuda back to headquarters. When we were able to round the horses up, we were supposed to move them down to a big, wide ford if the river was up. But we were anxious to get in and get our money.

Buddy knew the country and thought we could cross where we were camped. He said when we got close to the river, he would lope up to the bank and see if the water was low enough to swim it. He said if we could cross, we could get a lot of speed up. I guess he thought it

Buster Welch, right, with Tom McGuane and Red

would be like a car hitting a mud hole. So he went on and pretty soon I saw him coming back and waving his hat to come on. There were about seventy-five horses. When we got those suckers running and hit that river, probably twenty of them got downstream before the others stopped. We were lucky we didn't drown any of them. About dark, we got down to that ford where we should have gone in the first place and most of the horses had crossed there ahead of us.

So we got to San Angelo and were having fun. Those folks in town were glad to see us with fresh money. We were talking about what all we were going to buy, but when our money was all gone we hadn't even bought a new lace leather to fix a saddle.

We got pretty hungry and Buddy saw an old boy that he recognized and he told me to keep my mouth shut and he'd get us a piece of pie and a cup of coffee. So he walked over to this old boy and asked if he had any horses he needed ridden. He said, "Sure, are you boys huntin' a job?" Buddy said, "Yeah, buy us a piece of pie and a cup of coffee and we'll talk about it."

So he bought us a piece of pie and a cup of coffee and started talk-ing about his horses. We could see it was a pretty tough situation, and he needed good hands. To hear Buddy tell it, you would have thought on our last job we had to roll a cigarette on a bucking horse and not spill any tobacco. We were so good, in fact, we had to quit because we didn't want to get to smoking.

I was sitting there squirming, and Buddy made a date to go out at four o'clock the next morning. When he left, I said, "Buddy, if he don't have some horses that'll buck us off, he'll go buy some." Buddy said, "He don't have to buy some; he's got 'em. Buster, I didn't say we were going to ride his horses. I just said I'd get us a piece of pie and a cup of coffee."

We got a Greyhound bus back to the ranch instead. When we got there, everyone had gone to town. We waited and waited and final-ly Buddy said, "Let's fix these guys."

So we took the girths off their saddles and hid them. Then we unrolled their beds and put crackers and salt in them and rolled them back up.

We were afraid to walk back down the road to the highway for fear they would see us. So we cut across two or three miles and went to hitchhiking. We were afraid to ever ask what happened. We just cleared on out of the country.

When you first left home, you went to work for the Proctors. Tell us some more about them.

I went to work breaking horses during the war. I was nearly four-teen years old. All the qualified men were in the Army, so I went to work for them breaking horses. The Proctors were great men. They both had some college education. Their granddad was a captain in the Confederate cavalry, and after the war he came West.

He was primarily a horse-raiser. They settled south of Midland, and I've worked a lot of cattle on that home place. Both of them were great athletes. Foy had the best judgment. All my life, I've thought, "Now what would Foy Proctor do?"

I was real impressed with their good attitude. If it was real hot and somebody complained, Foy would say, "Yeah, it's nice and warm."

But the thing that impressed me most, we were moving a herd of cattle up close to Midland. We passed their mother's house. It sat nearly a half-mile off the road. I noticed her walking and carrying a big ten-gallon milk can. She was up in her late eighties then.

She caught water from the windmill for us to drink. Leonard offered to carry the can for her and she'd say, "Oh, no, you stay with those cattle, Leonard."

Once I described Foy as saying he could replace Charles Goodnight at any time or he would be leading the pack today. He was twenty or thirty years ahead of his time, and I didn't realize it when I was young.

I remember in 1979 all of a sudden the market went through the ceiling. A guy offered us $1 a pound for those steers, and I wanted to take it. All the young guys were saying, "Don't take it, it's going to $1.50."

I called Foy. He said, "Buster, I've never sold steer cattle for a dollar, but I sure would like to." He never said another word about it. He just dropped it. When we hung up, I called that guy immediately and traded.

Foy wouldn't elaborate or try to convince you, but I read later he had sold his, too. Then cattle got down to about 80 cents. Before it quit falling, those same cattle were selling for 55 cents.

Tell us how you got Mr. San Peppy.

Bubba Cassio called me when he was working for Mr. Howell. He had a colt that kept bucking the jockeys off, and he wanted me to take him and ride him two or three months. He thought ranch work would do him good. Bubba understood cutting horses better than anybody I knew when we were getting started.

He said the smartest thing one day when we were sitting around the kitchen table. We were talking about who was going to be successful at cutting, and he said the guy who learns how to train a good horse without ruining him on sour cattle. And, boy, that's the key.

I told him to send that colt on down that nobody could ride. He sent a real good jockey with him, and I wondered why. I figured that horse must really be bad. The jockey left along about the middle of the evening, and then I saddled the horse.

Boy, he could buck. I'd try to work him, but he was so full of energy and fired up I'd just send Rod back to lope him in those steep, rocky hills for an hour. He'd bring him back, and if he wasn't right I'd send him back again.

The final deal came one day when I wasn't paying attention. I was just going to raise my leg out and punch him in the girth. He felt my leg go out, and he ducked and that brought that spur right into his shoulder, and that scoundrel just ducked back under my left leg and started bucking.

He hit the fence and fell. When he came up, I rode him a little bit to make sure he wasn't hurt, and I don't think he ever humped up again.

I guess Bubba got busy and didn't want to fool with him. So Greg rode him in the futurity, and I rode Dry Dock and won the futurity on him.

Mr. Howell called me later and said he needed to sell the horse. I talked to Jay Agnew and told him I bet Mr. Howell wanted $25,000 for the horse. Turned out he wanted $50,000.

Jay was traveling in Europe, and I couldn't get hold of him, so I decided to go it myself and buy him.

For a long time after that I'd wake up at five o'clock in the morning and say, "Fifty thousand dollars!" Next morning, it would be four o'clock and the next morning at three o'clock. But shortly after I got him I rode him at a cutting and Matlock Rose came out to the trailer and offered to buy him. I figured then I had made a pretty good deal.

(Interviewed in 1995)

BOOTS O'NEIL

I cherish each time I get to ride with Boots O'Neil. Not only do I get to hear a lot of interesting cowboy stories, but I get to watch an unbelievable cowboy at work. I don't suppose you could go anywhere in Texas, Oklahoma, or New Mexico and find a cowboy who either didn't know or hadn't heard of Boots O'Neil. His reputation as the consummate cowboy has spread all over the cow country. Boots loves to tell stories and his memory is a as sharp as it was when he was a teenager. I'm proud to call him friend, and I'll see him at the Four Sixes in the spring. In the meantime, I'll join you, the reader, as Boots tells us about where he came from.

I grew up in the Texas Panhandle on the Davis Ranch out of Lefors in Gray County. I left there when I was seventeen and went to work for the JA Ranch, which was the old Goodnight estate in Palo Duro Canyon.

We had twelve or thirteen line camps and worked with a thirteen or fourteen-man wagon crew year-round. They pulled out a wagon in April when the grass would handle the horses. We'd pull the chuck wagon with four big horses, and we had a bed wagon and a water wagon. We'd pull them with single teams. The bed wagon had two old bucking horses we broke to work.

They would stay out until the horses started getting weak, along in November whenever the grass was fading.

Boots O'Neil

There's a lot of romance about the wagon, and all of us who would like to think we could live that kind of life don't really realize how tough that life was.

In looking back, it's hard for me to imagine we stayed two and three months out there. You couldn't even have a bag for clothes. Everything you had had to be in that bed when you rolled it up and loaded the wagon. They had to haul that stuff with wagons and teams. They didn't even have a pickup on the whole ranch. You had to go with a wagon team or on horseback. In all the years I worked there, I never seen a JA horse on wheels.

They had one of the best systems. They operated it just like they did when Colonel Goodnight was there. We'd make a drive in a big pasture with hundreds and hundreds of cows. We'd cut the bull calves out of one side of that herd and the heifers the other side. We had two traps, and we would take the heifers to one pasture and the bull calves to the other one. Anything left in that roundup that didn't mate up, you turned them loose and left them.

Every two or three days, we'd take bull calves out on top near Claude and work 'em and then ride back that night to the wagon. We always worked the heifers in the canyon because they claimed after you worked the bull calves, they wouldn't walk out, but the heifers would.

I remember when I was a kid we were going to move the wagon from one place to another. They usually put some new kid driving the bucking horses with the bed wagon. We were going right down the bed of the river. I was sitting up on top of like fourteen or fifteen bedrolls driving those horses.

We'd leave out with the chuck wagon, then the water wagon, and then the bed wagon. We had the remuda, and every time we crossed that channel they'd drive them horses across and back two or three times. We'd jump in and try to cross behind them.

I was trying to roll a Bull Durham cigarette up on top of those beds and dropped those lines. Those two old bucking horses started running and that old cook hollered, "Jump off, son, jump off." And I did. They turned that wagon over and it dumped those beds in the water and tore that harness up. I was reasonably sure they'd fire me, but they never said a word. It never was mentioned to me.

When you went to work for the JAs, like most ranches, they'd give you a slip of paper with your mount of horses on it. They issued you a stake rope, and every man staked a horse every night that he was going to ride on the drive the next morning. All the horses were broke to stake, and you had to move every night to get on fresh grass. If you staked him in the same place every night, he didn't have any supper or breakfast.

We just staked them by the neck, and some of them weren't gentle. You'd four-foot him and tie him down, and he'd try to bite you. We'd just leave him up hooked to a good, big saddle horse and drag him out there and stake him.

Even overnight, they'd fight all night. They were four-year-olds, and you had to have a crew of men to just pen them. It was just man against beast.

We don't break horses the same way today we did then, do we?

No, it's a lot better now. At that time I worked with some great men, and they just believed that's the way you done it—you just saddled a horse and got on him. Most of them bucked the first few saddles.

At the JAs, we just rode a bronc five times—two in the corral and three outside—then took him to the wagon. They never did really get gentle, even the good, top ranch horses.

Boots, you worked for the Waggoners for a long time. The ranch near Vernon is one of the most famous in Texas. When did you go there?

I went to work for the Waggoners in the fall of '52 on their ranch in New Mexico. They had a lot of horses that could buck, and I went there for that reason. I left after two or three months when I was asked if I wanted to help unload some oats. Nowadays I would, but then I told them I would rather go back to Texas than unload oats.

They encouraged me not to leave over it, but I thought I should either help unload the oats or leave, so I left about five o'clock in the evening. About ten or eleven o'clock that night I stopped for a cup of coffee, and the wagon boss of the Matadors was in there. I went to work for them the next morning.

The board of the Matadors was in Dundee, Scotland, from the start to the finish. They had the ranch at Matador, but the one I worked on was near Channing. When I left the Matador, I went to the Army, and when I came out of the Army in 1955 I went to the Waggoners, which is probably one of the biggest cow outfits that ever operated in modern times.

They had in the neighborhood of eight hundred sections and run from twelve to fourteen thousand mother cows. We used to try to keep three hundred broke geldings for saddle horses. I worked there twenty-four years and was the ranch foreman the last seven years I was there.

They had lots of horses that bucked and liked it. The oldtimers liked their horses to buck, and they encouraged it.

I worked from '55 to 1960, and I stayed at the wagon with the exception of two months in the winter of '57 when I stayed in the bronc camp and broke broncs.

They tell the story that W.T. Waggoner was seventeen years old when his daddy sent him up the trail with a load of Longhorns. He said his daddy bought the worst horses he could find, and he swore that when he got his own ranch he was going to have the finest horses in America, and by golly he did. The Waggoner-bred horses are still a very important part of the bloodlines of some of the finest horses we have in America today.

Right, the main bloodlines of the modern Quarterhorse originated at the Waggoners. We used to keep 225 brood mares and twenty-two or twenty-three stallions.

I have always thought the perfect image of a Quarterhorse was Poco Bueno, and I bet you got to ride a bunch of Poco Bueno colts, didn't you?

Yes, I rode many of them. In the heyday of the ranch we never did have Poco Bueno out there. Mr. Waggoner had him at a separate place to breed show horses. We had several great sons of Poco Bueno that we used throughout their lives.

Do you know where the mares came from?

No, I don't. When I first went to work there in '55, they were just getting the horses registered. None of those mares were halter broke, and they were really hard to handle. But they had tremendous mares.

There's got to be some funny stories that happened at the Waggoner Ranch. Can you think of one in particular?

I can think of an incident that I was told about that happened quite a bit before my time. Guy and Paul Waggoner, who were brothers, were left at the wagon to try to learn the business. At that time, money was a lot different. Rich people traveled the world. These boys had cars, and they weren't really interested in punching cows at that chuckwagon.

The wagon boss was trying to instill in them a little about the business, and the story is that a maverick bull broke out of the herd. This boy running the wagon hollered at Paul, "Head him, Paul, he's going to hell." Paul said, "Let him go. If he gets down there, Grandpa will get him!"

Let's talk about your life at the Waggoner as a foreman.
Tell us about some of the changes you saw in the industry.

What I've credited as the biggest change is roads. When I got there, there were a lot of places you couldn't go, but now they have roads.

During my time there, we had to start vaccinating the cows, and I think that's due to transportation. Cattle are so mobile now, and they spread a lot of diseases.

In the first year I was there, they just turned them out on the theory that if she didn't make it, you didn't want her.

We started calving heifers and started feeding a lot more cattle. They also launched the biggest program I've ever been in, cleaning the brush out. Probably the biggest detriment to the ranching industry in this country is brush and the control of it.

What are you doing now?

I work for the Four Sixes Ranch in Guthrie. A few years ago the owner and the manager wanted to have their own brand inspector, a man who was certified by the state of Texas as a legal peace officer. I was living in Vernon at that time working for myself, and they came down to talk to me.

The reason they chose me, as I understand, was for my background. They wanted somebody who could help them punch cows and just be an asset. I had worked for the Texas and Southwestern Cattle Raisers Association from 1960 to '64 as a field inspector and had that experience. So my wife and I moved here in February 1990.

We usually think of rustlers from the old days of the West, but we still have that problem, don't we?

Quite a bit. The cattle raisers association just recently made a case that involved two or three men and fifteen or sixteen cows. During the time I worked for them, I was instrumental and worked with local law enforcement on eleven cow theft cases where we tried them and got a conviction.

I stopped in Stamford one night about eleven o'clock to fill up with gas and saw a spot of blood on the driveway. Nowadays you'd think of murder, but then you didn't. The attendant said a fellow just filled up with gas and blood dripped out of the trunk of his car. I asked him if he knew who it was, and he gave me a name of a boy in Haskell County.

I went on to Haskell and got the sheriff up. We went out there, and this boy was cutting the beef up on the kitchen table. He had shot it in a little feed lot in Stamford and cut the hind quarters off him.

You're a great storyteller, so let's just sit back and you tell us some stories you remember.

I'm reminded of a story about Bill Cole that happened at the Waggoner Ranch. A carpenter was at the camp to work on a screen door. Bill was riding off horseback and told the carpenter to go ahead and work.

Bill was out away from the house, and a stud came running at him out of the brush. Bill whirled to run and was running wide open. The stud ran into his horse and grabbed him by the leg and jerked him off and tore the muscle off his leg.

The stud horse ran Bill's saddle horse plum out of the country. It broke Bill's leg, and he laid there most of the day. About five o'clock that evening, the carpenter told the boys Bill never came back. They got in a helicopter and found him. He was nearly dead and never did really get over it.

He had taken his shirt off and stuffed grass in it and wrapped it around his leg to stop the bleeding.

I don't know that I've ever told you the story about the time when we had all those big steers tied to the trees on the river and it came a flood. This was in the middle '50s. We were catching big steers out of the Dead Man pasture.

We had several big steers up and down the river. We were going back the next day. We'd lead them out to where we could load them. A big flash flood came through and drowned several of the steers.

For many years afterward, on the down water side, you'd find the big horns tied to the tree with the skeleton and all. Now then, they'd be lined up down there to get those skulls.

One time back in the '50s, I had a brand new Bob Marrs saddle. We were working during a lot of rains and crossing Beaver Creek. It was up and would swim a horse.

G.L. Proctor was running the wagon. A bunch of us were there, and we were going to try to get across Beaver Creek.

It was up pretty big. A big cottonwood tree had fallen across it, and one man tried to go across on the limb and get on the other side. We tied two lariat ropes together and tied bridle reins in the end of the rope and throwed it across the river.

Just the strength of man holding it would keep the horse straight. He would swim across the river. We'd put it right under our armpits and jump in, and he would lead us across.

But my horse got loose and went down the river a good ways and climbed out in another pasture. My saddle was brand new, and it got totally soaked in that old red mud. I heard just a year or two ago that Bob Marrs got to telling people about that saddle when I brought it back in to clean up. It was really a mess.

I've got two stories in mind that happened with me and Manford Elliott. He's a retired brand inspector for the Texas and Southwestern Cattle Raisers Association. At the time he was working for the Waggoner Ranch, and I was working there. It involves me and the same two horses. I was riding a horse called Black Jack, and he was riding a horse called Chaparita.

I don't remember if Chaparita bucked Manford off or fell, but he came down through there loose. I ran up on that thing and roped him by the saddle horn. When he hit the end of it, this horse I was riding just blowed up, and I bailed out.

Those two horses went through there tearing down trees, saddle horn to saddle horn. When we caught up with them down there on the creek, they were facing one another on the end of that rope like a calf-roping horse. Their ol' ears was just working, looking at one another. We eased up there and took the ropes off of them and went on and finished the drive.

Another time, we were up there at Cedar Top in the canyon catching big steers. Chaparita got loose again and just came out of them cedars coming by me, and I roped that scamp again. He hit the end of that thing and jerked old Black Jack down and we had a pretty good wreck there.

That was in a period of two or three years. It was the same two men and the same two horses, and we were probably within forty miles of where it happened the first time.

I remember a story when Donald Hatfield had just retired from the Waggoners and moved into Electra. He and I were going down the road with two horses in a trailer and met a little old bull. I said, "There's a dadgum maverick bull that's got out of the North Red."

We unloaded and caught that scamp and castrated him and hauled him into the ranch. The boss told us to take him to the sale. We took him to Wichita and sold him because he wasn't branded.

We found out three or four days later he was a little registered bull that had got away from the preacher and was coming down that lane. I knew the preacher real well, and he was a good friend.

I traced the bull around and found him in a feedlot. I talked to the ranch manager and told him I could catch two little old maverick heifers on the creek and satisfy him and get us out of trouble. That's what we did.

Tell us the story about Shinnery McElroy.

The Indians had captured him like so many out of that Wise County country when it was the frontier. They had him for two or three years, and Mr. Waggoner supposedly traded horses for him when they had cattle in the Oklahoma Territory.

The story is that he could run so fast that he could outrun all the Indian boys, so the Indians cut a ligament in his knee. He walked with a limp the rest of his life.

The Waggoners raised him, and he worked for them throughout the rest of his life and raised a family there. He was kind of a foreman and lead-off man for the Waggoners for years and years.

Robert McElroy was his son. I worked with him for years and years. He died back in the '70s. He has a son, Bob, that lives in Crowell now.

Until about 1874, the western part of civilization in Texas was Weatherford, which is only about thirty miles west of Fort Worth. That was really the frontier. They had threats of Indians every single day. A lot of them died from disease that could have been treated had they been living now. It was a pretty tough life.

There's a little grave on the Waggoners that's on the edge of a creek. The story was that a family had homesteaded back in there, and a little boy got sick. They were going to Seymour to a doctor and got to a creek that they couldn't cross. They had to wait two or three hours and this boy died and they just buried him right there.

Some sixty or seventy years later, some folks from Pennsylvania came to the ranch that was part of that family. They took a nice monument over there with his birth date and a little epitaph. It's just out in a pasture with no fence there.

(Interviewed in 1995)

JOAQUIN JACKSON

I have known Joaquin Jackson for quite some time. I honestly believe that if you ask an artist to paint a picture of a Texas Ranger, it would be a portrait of Joaquin Jackson. He's one of the most interesting people I have ever met. Not only has he had a varied career, but everyone who knows him just thinks he is one of the finest gentlemen they've ever known.

Joaquin upheld his duties as a Texas Ranger in the true style in which this elite law enforcement agency was designed. He truly is a Texas treasure and I'm proud to call him my friend. As with all of my other guests, I just had to know about Joaquin's background. Here's what he had to say:

I was born in my grandfather's farmhouse in Lamb County northeast of Anton on Nov. 12, 1935. My grandfather had come from the Granger area and started farming when they broke out the old Spade Ranch into farm areas and sold them. He bought a half-section of land. My dad was a farmer, and I grew up on a farm.

When I was in high school and my father was farming, I worked on what was left of the Spade Ranch with an old cowboy named Joe Christopher. I'd get up early in the morning and get out there about five.

Mrs. Christopher would have breakfast ready, and Joe would pour about three fingers of Old Crow in a glass and drink it like you and I would drink orange juice before breakfast. He kept bottles hidden around the ranch, but you never saw him drunk. He did a day's worth of work. He was a good man and a good hand.

Joaquin Jackson

I played basketball at West Texas State University, but I didn't graduate. I joined the Highway Patrol in 1957, and while I was going through the DPS academy, a Ranger captain talked to us.

That was the first time I knew anything about the Rangers. I made up my mind then I'd like to get in the Ranger service. It sounded like the kind of job I wanted where you had a lot of freedom of movement.

I went on the road the first of August 1957. I was stationed in Brownfield and Littlefield and then went to Jacksboro for three years. I went into the Ranger service the first of April 1966. Captain A.Y. Allee hired me to be stationed in Uvalde.

The first day I went to work for Captain Allee there was an uprising of sorts down in Carrizo Springs and he called me down there. Some guys had overpowered the jailer and taken all the guns to the second floor of the jail building and were shooting at anybody that tried to come close to the jail.

When I walked up to Captain Allee, he told me to get down. He then called up to the guys on the second floor and said, "I'll give you to the count of ten to throw down your arms and come out." He counted, "One, two, three" and started shooting.

I said, "Captain, you didn't count to ten." He said, "Hell, Joaquin, they can't count."

I recall Captain Allee came from an old tradition that expected seven days of work for pay. I was making around $750 a month, and we worked anywhere from ninety to a hundred and twenty hour weeks.

We'd get off on Sunday until noon and then do follow-up investigations on homicides, burglaries or cattle thefts or whatever. That was the old tradition of the Rangers. We worked and stayed busy. That's one of the things that's built the Rangers to what it is. They're a hard-working organization.

After Captain Allee retired we had the start of La Raza Unida Party in Crystal City. Jose Angel Gutierrez was the leader of it. It was a coming thing because the county was probably eighty to eighty-five percent Mexican-American, and the government was controlled mostly by Anglos.

When the La Raza Unida movement hit, I developed a pretty good rapport with Jose Angel Gutierrez and was able to talk to both sides.

Through these negotiations, I think we probably stopped some bloodshed or bad deals.

On election day, they called us to the old county barn where the election was being held. There were probably 500 to 600 Mexican-Americans across the highway from the election place.

Jose Angel Gutierrez and his wife were there. She and another lady wanted to be poll watchers, so we walked over to the election place. The election judge was an attorney and had the same authority as a district judge on election day.

He said he wanted the women removed from the building. They wouldn't get up, so we carried them in their chairs out onto the front porch.

Jose saw us and said he wanted to talk to us. He had an election code and pointed out to me they were allowed two poll watchers per candidate. They probably had 30 candidates, but they just asked for two poll watchers for all the candidates. We settled that dispute and they all left.

I turned to the election judge and told him they were allowed two people per candidate but were only asking for two poll watchers. He said he wouldn't allow them in and I said, "Okay, but you're on your own."

We started walking off, and he said, "Wait a minute, wait a minute, you can let them back in."

Through those situations, I kept good relations. Anglos and Hispanics were both carrying guns in their vehicles. Later on after it died down, one of his bodyguards told me Gutierrez had told him, "If that Ranger gets here, don't let him get to his trunk because he's got everything in the world in there."

> ***There was a young man that you helped out one time that the world got to know, and I want the world to know that story from your point of view.***

You're talking about Johnny Rodriguez. He was a fine young man and a great talent. I was in Uvalde about 1969 or 1970. Lots of people came to Garner State Park in the summer. Johnny was from Sabinal, and he'd come to the park and pick and sing.

The first time I saw him we were coming up to the park entrance and saw someone laying out by the road passed out. I punched him with my boot. He jumped up and said he was okay. We drove him to where he was staying in the park, and the next time I saw him he was in the county jail. He got arrested for stealing a registered Angora goat and barbecuing it.

One night after he got out of jail for that, I stopped by the jail where I had a prisoner or two. The sheriff told me Johnny was back in jail, and I asked him if he had ever heard him sing. He said he hadn't, so I went back to the house and got a guitar to bring to the jail.

Johnny tuned it and sang for about an hour, one song right after another. A lot of them he wrote. The sheriff was really impressed and told Johnny he would let him out and he could bring him the money when he got some work.

I later introduced him to Happy Shahan at Alamo Village. Tom T. Hall and some others came down on Labor Day the second year he was there and got acquainted with Johnny. They wanted him to come to Nashville, but Happy said he wasn't stage-ready. Later that winter Johnny got tired of waiting around and took off on his own for Nashville.

Tom T. called Happy and me looking for him, and they finally got hold of him in a motel in Nashville. Tom T. got him a contract with Mercury and they did *Pass Me By*.

Johnny was doing great. Then he got out to California and people would take him to their house. They set cocaine out on the table, and that stuff got a hold of him. From there on, it was downhill, but for five years Johnny was at the top.

He dried out a couple of times, but of course, he later got involved in a homicide in Sabinal and faced the possibility of going to the penitentiary for life.

He was a great person. I never saw him violent. He reminded me of a young Will Rogers. Nobody ever met Johnny who didn't like him. He had a great personality.

How long did you stay around Uvalde?

I was there twenty-one years and then transferred to Alpine in 1987. In 1968 I was sent to Brownsville in Cameron County to work on some oil field thefts. A couple of brothers were stealing mercury out of meters in the oil patch and selling it to an old fellow down south of Alpine who was reselling it as mined mercury.

We busted that ring. After I arrested them, I had them in the county jail. The next morning about seven o'clock I was over at the courthouse and ran into a young lawyer who was representing them. In those days you could go over to the jail and talk to them. So that afternoon I went over to the jail and got a confession from those two boys.

Since this young lawyer had been such a nice fellow, I carried copies of the confessions by his office and left them. Later we recovered the stolen mercury and arrested the guy for fencing it.

After several years went by, I got a letter from that young lawyer, and he had become a Methodist preacher. He related that story and said the next morning he went into the office and his secretary handed him that confession. He had told them not to make a confession. He immediately visualized they were going to have black eyes and missing teeth, and they were going to be all beat up.

He got in there and there wasn't a mark on them. He said, "Did you give that Ranger a confession?" They said, "Yes sir, we couldn't help it. He was the nicest fellow we ever talked to."

Tell us some more about the Rangers.

A Ranger's job is to do criminal investigation work for the state of Texas. There are six Ranger companies, A through F headquartered in Houston, San Antonio, Waco, Midland, Lubbock, and Dallas.

When I came in there were six or eight men per Ranger company. Now there's something like fifteen or eighteen. When I came in there was sixty-five Rangers in the state, and now there's a hundred and five, and they tell me they need more.

The Rangers were established unofficially in 1823 by Stephen F. Austin. He hired ten men out of his own pocket to protect the settlers from marauding Indians. In 1835 the Rangers were officially organized as a group. At that time they were more of a militia for the Republic of Texas.

They were organized as law enforcement in 1875 when they became peace officers. This worked on down until the creation of the Department of Public Safety in 1935. They put the Highway Patrol and the Rangers in the DPS. Walter Prescott Webb said in his book, 'This will be the end of the Texas Rangers." Fortunately, it wasn't.

In 1937 Homer Garrison took them under his arm and developed them in to the modern crime fighting organization they are today.

The Ranger service has existed ever since 1835 officially. They're well over a hundred years old, and I think they'll be here as long as we've got a state of Texas.

Basically the Rangers are most effective in rural areas with smaller police departments where they're not as well trained as the Rangers are. The sheriff's department will call us in to assist them.

After we get established in an area, the victims of crimes get to know you. They'll call us, and I'll call the sheriff to keep good working relations.

Another thing they end up doing is special investigations that have to do with politicians. The reason for that is the Rangers are less politically controlled than any other organizations, and they can work without their hands being tied.

Tell us about some of the Rangers you admire.

Lone Wolf Gonzaullas became a Ranger captain, but he was a private when he cleaned up some of the towns in East Texas during the oil boom. He was a great man and respected by citizens of this state. I never met the man but would have liked to.

Another Ranger I admire greatly is Frank Hamer. I've probably read more on him than any Ranger. He was hired by the prison system and commissioned to track down Bonnie and Clyde. They had brutally murdered two Highway Patrolmen, and Hamer tracked them down and killed them. But he was well known for a lot of other things besides Bonnie and Clyde.

At one time there was a five thousand dollar reward to get anyone who attempted a bank robbery, so that set off a series of corrupt officials. They would get some local drunk and have him be in front of a bank at nine o'clock on some morning, and they'd blow him away and the banker and law enforcement would split the money.

So Frank got into that. He got into a shootout over in Sweetwater one time. His wife was in the car, and she shot and killed a guy coming up behind Frank.

Joaquin, as a historian of the Texas Rangers, what does it mean to you to have served as a Texas Ranger rather than to have served as a Highway Patrolman? Both do a tremendous service to the people of the state of Texas.

Well, I served nine years in the Highway Patrol, and that's probably the most dangerous job because the unexpected is what gets an officer killed. Of course, a lot of times, you tend to go toward complacency. You'll think it's just a routine stop and then get blown away by some guy who just killed his family or pulled a robbery you didn't get word on.

The Ranger service to me is the greatest law enforcement organization in the world and running second to it would probably be the Royal Canadian Mounted Police. They were built through hard work, they do their duty, and aren't bribed or corrupt. I hope it continues that way, and I'm sure it will.

The nine years I spent in the Highway Patrol, I wouldn't take for that. It's an entirely different job. It's traffic supervision. The Ranger service is a little bit more freedom. You don't have as much supervision.

Tell us the story of Captain McNelly.

He probably was one of the greatest Ranger captains we ever had. He was a Civil War veteran, and he had what they called consumption, which we know as TB today.

He came into Texas after the Civil War. During the Reconstruction period, the Rangers were done away with for four or five years. There was a state police, and he served on it. When they re-created the Rangers, they made him a captain. He made up a battalion and was working out in West Texas fighting the Indians in 1874 and 1875.

He was sent down to the Nueces Strip with a battalion of men. They had tried it before but had always been spotted. So McNelly hired a man named Crazy Juan or something like that. His family had been killed by the Mexican bandits, so he had a bitter hatred toward them.

McNelly hired him as a Ranger and made him a guide. He would interrogate them and then hang them. A lot of people would say that was awfully brutal, but that's the way they lived in those days. It was kill or be killed.

McNelly moved through that country silently and put a stop to the killing and stealing. He even went so far as to invade Mexico after 140 head of the King Ranch cattle.

He hit the wrong hacienda the first time. They next time they encountered about four hundred Mexicans, who stayed on the Mexican side and kind of dug in. They had a standoff and he told them he would leave Mexico when they brought him the 140 head of cattle.

He popped one of the Mexican lieutenants across the head with a pistol and said, "Now I'll give you your lieutenant back when you bring me my cattle."

In the meantime, he got a letter from the United States government saying he had invaded a foreign country and to get out of there. He sent a letter back to them and said, "I don't work for the federal government. I work for the state of Texas, and I'll get out of Mexico when my job's done." The bandits finally brought the 140 head of cattle and even crossed the river for him.

He died in his early thirties. The year before, the state had laid him off because they didn't want to pay his medical bills.

Let's talk a little bit about Rangering in West Texas, where you live now.

I transferred to Alpine after serving twenty-one years in Company D in Uvalde. When I came to Alpine I was in Company E, headquartered in Midland. Captain Gene Powell was my commander.

When I got out there I spent a lot of long hours learning the country and the people. There was a lot of drug smuggling along the river, and I developed spies or informants. They would give more information to a man wearing a Ranger badge than any other badge.

One of the most infamous shootings happened with some rafters in November 1989. A man and his wife and a river guide started down the river and came into smoke in the canyon. Four boys had come in and set fire to brush in an old marijuana field. These guys were up on the canyon ridge wall and started shooting at a Hereford that was on the U.S. side. In a little bit they saw the raft coming and one of them hollered out, "Let's shoot the gringos."

They started shooting at the raft and hit it two or three times. The guide took a .22 round to his thigh. They crouched down in some boulders and probably would have been okay if they had stayed there. But they started on down the river and came to some rock outcroppings and had to get in the water.

The boys on the ridge were following them and shooting at them. When they got to the last outcropping, the woman took a round in her side from a .30-.30. Her husband was helping her out of the water, and he took a .44 magnum round through the back.

He fell down, and she lay there and watched him die. Finally she got up and went over next to the bluff on the Texas side and got in some brush and hid there. Later that night, people from the rafting company came looking for them and found the raft with holes shot in it. They went down through there hollering and she heard them, but she was so frightened she didn't even answer them.

The sheriff called me at 3 A.M., and when I got down there they had called in the Border Patrol and customs. We got down the river to the crime scene and found the man's body. We got the woman to the hospital in a helicopter and then got hold of the Mexico state police. We went over to Mexican side and started tracking. We found signs of two mules and two horses and then found the camp where they were.

When we got back to the U.S. side I knew the Mexicans weren't going to pursue it. So I went to the U.S. Border Patrol chief in Marfa and asked if we could put up roadblocks on either side of Redford. I knew the drug dealers in Redford would give us the names within ten days because they knew we were going to cut their business off.

We found one of the shooters in a house, but the other three were gone. He said he was there but didn't shoot anybody. He finally said he did some shooting but didn't hit anybody.

We found his gun and tied it in with ballistics. We ended up in Chihuahua City with the other three, but we never got them back across the river to try them. We tried the other one, and he got thirty years in the penitentiary.

(Interviewed in 1999)

BUCK TAYLOR

Buck Taylor has been a very special friend of mine for over 30 years. I have watched him grow as a painter to be one of the most prominent artists in America. The world has watched him grow as an actor to be one of the greatest actors of his time. The people who are fortunate enough to call him friend love him dearly and know without a shadow of a doubt, that he is one of the kindest, most talented, most giving people that any of us have ever known. I am deeply honored to be counted among his friends.

Buck has a very interesting background.His dad was a fabulous character actor and Dub wore a pretty large pair of shoes, but Buck has done a good job of filling them. It's interesting to know where Buck came from and how he grew up, so that's where we began.

I want to start with where you came from. You grew up in a unique society that not many people know anything about.

I look back through my life and I realize I grew up in a dream world. My dad was an actor. He came to Hollywood from vaudeville. I happened to be born in Hollywood during film testing. I was born in an apartment building at the corner of Hollywood and Western, which turned out to be appropriate.

From there we moved to the San Fernando Valley. I grew up knowing Wild Bill Elliott and Tex Ritter—they were friends of my dad. I look back now and realize how fortunate I was.

In those days, the studios for the Westerns were the ranches. I would sneak in them as a kid and wander around. I never thought

Buck Taylor

much of it at the time, but I grew up around top professional cowboys and cowgirls from all over the country.

I was surrounded by this wealth of flavor of the West. It was awesome when you think about it. I was very fortunate.

Were you on a lot of movie sets in those early days?

Yeah, I would go with my dad occasionally. He'd turn me loose and I would run up and down the streets on a stick horse. It was a fantasy world.

I loved my mom and dad, too. They taught me the principles and values and honor that seems to be slipping away, but I think we can get it back.

I was very fortunate to know both your parents. Your dad kind of adopted me after we became friends, which has been a long, long time. He was a wonderful human being.

He was a great guy, and later in life I really got to know him after my mom passed away. I got divorced, so he was single and I was single. I thought I knew him, and then I really got to know him.

Let's talk about some of those people you mentioned a while ago. Tex Ritter was one of my heroes. I just absolutely idolized him.

Well, I did, too. My dad and him did a lot of crow hunting. They got twenty-five cents apiece for them, but I don't know if they ever collected. When I was a kid, I had a whole album of him. He sang great songs and had that country voice.

I also met Hank Williams when I was a kid. I went on the road with my dad and I met him in Louisiana. I've been so fortunate to meet people like that.

On one of our trips we went through Fort Worth, and I remember thinking this was a city but it was a Western city. I never dreamed I would be living here some day. Maybe that's why I am. You project yourself into where you want to be in life.

After I started coming to Texas, I just loved this country. Coming over here, I got to thinking of the romance of the West and the love I have for our history. What a colorful area of the United States we live in.

When was the first time you worked in a film?

My first movie was like 1959. I had gotten out of the service. I was going to try out for the Olympics, which I did in 1960. I was going to be a stuntman at the time. A friend of mine had become a great stuntman, so he kind of helped me get into it. It wasn't a Western I did, but *Rescue 8*, which I did with Jim Davis. That kind of launched my career.

I just finished a film called the *Wild, Wild West*, which is a comedy. Everybody wants to do Westerns, and I think we're going to see more of them.

It's kind of fascinating. You'll go on a movie set, and it never fails that the conversation always turns to John Wayne. I met him one time. We were doing *Gunsmoke*, and John Wayne was shooting a movie on the same lot. Glenn Strange, who was nicknamed "Pee Wee," offered to introduce me.

We walked in, and John Wayne says, "Pee Wee, how are you?" He introduced me as Dub Taylor's son, and Wayne said, "How ya doing, kiddo?" He shook my hand, and I don't know what he said after that.

I met Michael Wayne years later. In our conversations, we talked about our childhood. I was telling him how I would sneak into Republic Studios. John Wayne did a World War II movie called *Flying Tigers*. They had a fake Flying Tiger on the lot, and it just sat there after the movie was made. It didn't have a propeller or anything because it was a fake, but I used to sneak in there and climb in this plane and fly it.

I told Michael that and he said, "I did the same thing." We were both the same age. He's really a neat guy. John Wayne's family are wonderful people. That legacy will live with us forever. He was the man.

Most people recognize you as Newly from the* Gunsmoke *series.
How did you get into that?

I did my first TV show in 1959, and I didn't start *Gunsmoke* until 1967. I was in a number of shows like *Bonanza* and *Wagon Train* because I grew up around horses. I was hired in *Hang 'em High*. They offered me the part of Danno in *Hawaii Five-O*. I had been in

Gunsmoke, and they wanted me to play the part of Newly. So all those things were happening at once.

I got the test for *Gunsmoke,* I got the *Hang'em High,* and I had the part for *Hawaii Five-O,* so I asked my agent what I should do. He said *Gunsmoke* had been on the air twelve years and was a solid show. He didn't know if *Hawaii Five-O* would last and Eastwood would make another movie.

I said I would like to do *Gunsmoke* if I had a choice. I was so glad I did. I went on *Gunsmoke* in 1967, and ever since then it's been playing all over the world two or three times a week. When we did it, it was great.

I'm still getting a ride off it. It helped me with my artwork. The *Gunsmoke* fans were the first to support me with my paintings. I told Ken Curtis before he passed away that *Gunsmoke* fans were buying all my paintings. He told me, "Buck, enjoy the ride." And I have. It's been endless.

We've been lamenting the passing of the West since the turn of the century and yet the cowboy endures primarily because of people like you and the projects they're involved in. Of all the projects you were involved in, what would be the one that was most realistic to you?

I think *Tombstone,* historically, was not 100 percent accurate, but they really tried to do the wardrobe, the saddles, the horses, the speech of the period. I think that would have to rank up there for what I've done. It was so well done. I've been very proud of that. The *Sacketts* was pretty good, too.

I want you to stop and think about some of the funny things and impressive things that happened to you when you were on the Gunsmoke ***set. That was a part of our world for so long.***

There were so many of them. I wasn't there, but Doc—Milburn Stone—told us about Ken Curtis—Festus—signing autographs at a rodeo. They'd sit there until the last kid was gone. As you're signing things, you can start hearing conversations as people get closer to you.

Buck Taylor, center, with Jerry Potter and Red

Doc said a woman was talking to a little boy, and she kept saying, "Now you know who that is" as they were looking at Festus. They finally got right up in front of Festus and the boy's mother said, "Now who is that?" and the little boy said, "Jesus?"

I couldn't work with Jim Arness because he was so funny. He had this great sense of humor, and I could not look him in the eye. We'd be rehearsing a scene, and I would bust through the door and say, "There's a fight in the Long Branch," and he'd say, "Man, this guy's serious about doing this stuff."

And I was, and he'd get me laughing, but he wouldn't laugh. In the eight years I was on the show, I was never fully comfortable around Jim Arness. He was six foot, eight. He was Matt Dillon. I had watched him before I got on the show.

I would always have to pinch myself. I would be in the Long Branch and look around and here was Matt and Festus and Doc and Kitty. I would go, "Wow! And I'm here with them!"

When was the first time you met Ben Johnson?

My dad had talked about him forever and worked with him. I thought he was as close to the real thing that Hollywood had ever seen. I replaced a person in the TV series *The Monroes*. Ben was starring in it. I was the cattle boss of this outfit, and Ben played a guy with one arm. I told Ben I wanted him to help me if he saw me doing something that wasn't right. He got me all wardrobed out right. He was one of the neatest guys I ever met in my life. He was a dear friend of my dad's, and he taught me a lot."

Did you know Gene and Roy?

I met Gene Autry at the Cowboy Hall of Fame. I think they were honoring us for *Gunsmoke*. A lot of people knew him as the Singing Cowboy, but what a genius he was in business.

I'll never forget one time Roy Rogers went dove hunting with my dad. My dad was going over to friends' house to cook them, and he told me to wait and ride with Roy Rogers so I could tell him where they lived. So Roy came by in a Cadillac convertible, and I escorted him over there. It meant something to me then, but it means more to me now.

Let's talk a little bit about what's happening with you now.

I did a couple of movies. One was with Burt Reynolds, who worked on *Gunsmoke* before I did. Oddly enough, we were up for the same part. He played a guy named Quint Asper. He was a blacksmith. They wanted a half-breed Indian. I was Irish, and Burt had some Indian blood in him. Later I came on the show. We had met each other a few times, and he was always real nice to me.

I was constantly drawing as a little boy. I majored in art in school and got a scholarship to Chennard Art School in Los Angles. I went there and then to USC on an athletic scholarship. Then I went into the service, got out and then didn't paint for 30 years.

I started again with a fever. It's a love and a way for me to express myself. I had no idea when I started that it would afford me all I have. It's given me everything I've ever wanted. I even met my wife because of my artwork.

I've watched you grow as an artist, and you are so highly regarded.

It's really difficult. I look back on some of my earlier paintings, and I see a lot of things I don't like. I see some things I was doing right, and you try to hone it. I know I'm getting better because I want to get better. It's a labor of love.

Did you ever meet Walter Brennan?

Yes, I sure did. I was on the *Gunsmoke* set and I walked out by the sound stages. Walter Brennan was sitting out by himself and I said hello to him. We talked for about a half hour. He was a wonderful man and a tremendous actor.

I've worked with so many great character actors. Milburn Stone has to be one of my favorites.

I don't believe we've ever really talked about the people who make the movies work, the directors, the people behind the scenes.

It's the directors' film, their painting. They have to tell a story in a series of photographs on screen. It has to make sense, it has to jar imagination and involve us in this particular story. It starts with the written word and ends up on film, and it's difficult. John Ford might be the guide for any director to look at for Western movies.

We had a mutual friend, Bob Totten, who was certainly a protégé of John Ford films. He had the qualities that make a Western filmmaker. Recently I did a film with John Milius, who I think is a tremendous director.

He is known as the "script doctor" in Hollywood. People like Steven Spielberg will bring a script to him and say, "Fix this," and he will.

***What did you work in that Totten did? He was a task master, but
he was tougher on himself than he was on anybody else.***

Bob did put a lot of pressure on himself. He did fifty or so
Gunsmokes that were probably some of the best episodes. I did a film
with him called *Pony Express Rider.* He did *The Sacketts* and John
Steinbeck's *The Red Pony.*

***If you had to pick out one Western movie that you thought was the
best Western movie ever made, what would that be?***

That's a tough one. I guess the one that made the biggest impres-
sion on me might be *Fort Apache.* It's tough. *Red River* would be my
favorite cowboying movie, dealing with cattle.

I loved *Fort Apache* as a cavalry movie and the way John Ford
dealt with the Indians, giving them respect. I loved that movie. I
loved *The Cowboys* with John Wayne and those kids. *Lonesome Dove*
ranks up there with the best of them. I wish I had been in it. It's one
of my favorites.

***The Western movies and television shows are not a thing of the
past, but they don't have the major impact they used to have.***

John Wayne would do a lot of Westerns and then he would do
other shows. People would ask him how that differed from his
Westerns and he would say, "It's always John Wayne the cowboy no
matter what I do."

And it was. It was what he did.

(Interviewed in 1997)

INDEX